ROYAL
BLOOD

MARTIN O'CONNELL

HERO BOOKS

ROYAL
BLOOD

MARTIN O'CONNELL

With David Sheehan

www.**HERO**BOOKS.digital

www.gaffneymechanical.ie

HEROBOOKS

PUBLISHED BY HERO BOOKS
1 WOODVILLE GREEN
LUCAN
CO. DUBLIN
IRELAND

Hero Books is an imprint of Umbrella Publishing
First Published 2019
Copyright © Martin O'Connell 2019
All rights reserved

ISBN 9781910827109

Cover Design and formatting: Jessica Maile
Ebook formatting: www.ebooklaunch.com
Cover photograph: Inpho
Inside photographs: Inpho, Sportsfile, John Quirke and the O'Connell family collection

Dedication

To my parents

Paddy and Marie

Thanks for everything

ACKNOWLEDGEMENTS

'IT TAKES A village to raise a child' is an old African proverb and that's exactly what it takes to raise or produce a footballer. It starts with your family, your school friends and your local club. A huge amount of my success was down to the people around me in the early years.

My mother, Marie and my father Paddy. And my siblings, Marie, Doreen, Geraldine, Robert, Pat, Michael and David.

Then we have St Michael's GAA club. This is where I could be found most evenings, kicking a ball. There were people in that club who believed in me; they saw something in me that others didn't, and they made me believe in myself. This is where you start and end your career as a footballer - with your neighbours, friends and family. I will always be indebted to the club members in those early years when I was brought onto the county team as a minor and then senior. These men drove me to training and matches, near and far. Coming from a family of eight, the car was not always available for just me! These men followed my career and treated me like a king, and I will never forget them for it.

I thank my wife, Samantha for all the support over the years. Football, or any sport, can be a selfish business, but Samantha was there through thick and thin cheering me on, washing the gear or just listening to me moaning about my injuries. This was done with a smile and without complaint. She kept me grounded with her attitude of... 'It's only a game!'

Thanks to my children, Jane, Brian and Barry for listening to me as I waffle on about football or life 'in my day'. I train the two boys now with our local club, Walterstown GFC and I know at times I may be hard to listen to but I promise lads, it will all be worth it.

To my other family – all my teammates from club to county. I was blessed to play with such great lads. You were all like brothers to me. I shared some of the best moments of my life with you and it's something I will always cherish.

I owe a huge amount of debt to all my coaches, from underage upwards. I was coached by the best, and each and every one of those people taught me something useful that I could carry forward to the next stage.

I was extremely lucky while playing for Meath to be invited abroad to various functions. Thanks to all those loyal and kind GAA men and women in London, Canada and New York, to name but a few. I was treated so well on these excursions and, of course, we'd a bit of craic also!

My fellow parishoner and my clubmate in St Michael's, Niall Gaffney has been a generous sponsor of this story of my football life, and it is especially great to have one of our own and such a successful company as Gaffney Mechanical at my shoulder on this special occasion.

I have to single out one person though and that is Sean Boylan, as without Sean I feel there would be no All-Irelands, All Stars or any other awards or accolades. Sean was the glue that got all those lads together and turned them into men. He saw things in lads that others might not have seen. He had the vision and spotted raw talent from a mile off. There was no such thing as a finished product with Sean – he moulded lads into footballers.

You might play corner-forward with your club, but Sean might have you corner-back with the county as he could see that may be a better position for you. He has been a gentleman and a true friend to me, aswell as a brilliant manager.

Thank you, Sean.

Martin O'Connell,
October, 2019

❖ ❖ ❖ ❖ ❖ ❖ ❖ ❖

TAKING ON A task of this size, especially for the first time, doesn't leave much time for reflection during the writing process. Once the bulk of the work was done, however, I had time to think about what and whom had brought me to this point.

The fact that I have a large amount of (usually useless!) knowledge buried in my mind about Martin O'Connell and the Meath teams of the 1980s and 90s is due in large part to my parents, Eddie and Monica. Not only did they take me to Páirc Tailteann, Croke Park, Portlaoise and everywhere in between to watch Meath play, but they also made sure I had every Meath tracksuit and jersey under the sun when I was growing up. The phrase *'nothing beats being there'* is very common now, but it's something that I realised at an early age, when my fascination (some would say obsession) with Meath football took root, and has never left.

If that seed was sown by my parents, who encouraged me to play with my local club, then it was nurtured by some inspirational figures at Bective GFC. Great men such as John Moran, Gerry O'Grady, Mickey Morris, Tony Geraghty, Bobby Swatman, and Paddy McConnell – to name but a few – who at different times took on the role of coach, manager, bus driver and anything else that was necessary to ensure we got the most out of our underage football. This was at a very difficult time for what was then a new rural club. The fact that Bective can now hold their own at Intermediate level is the greatest tribute possible to the men and women who guided the club through those difficult early years and instilled a love of Gaelic football into my life.

I should also thank my brother, John for dragging me down to the pitch at a young age to kick the ball back out to him while he practiced his frees. I didn't know it at the time, but it taught me the value of hard work and practice, especially when I was fishing the wayward efforts out of the ditch!

I would also like to thank Eamonn Doyle, Brendan Cummins, Colm Corrigan, Gerry Kelly and everyone at *LMFM Radio*, who gave me the platform to talk about sport on a weekly basis, and to Cathal Dervan for suggesting my name when Liam Hayes was looking for someone to work with Martin on this project. It was probably a bit of a punt on Liam's part, but I'm so grateful for the opportunity and hopefully I haven't let him or Martin down.

To Samantha, Jane, Brian and Barry. Thanks for making me feel so welcome in your home, and for the plentiful supply of tea and biscuits every time I called to sit down with the man of the house.

Finally, of course, thanks to Martin for being so generous with his time and frank with his views. I grew up in awe of Martin and his teammates, so to have the opportunity to put his story into words was something I could never have hoped for when I was a 10-year-old fan.

An Mhí Abú.

David Sheehan,
October, 2019

❖ ❖ ❖ ❖ ❖ ❖ ❖

PROLOGUE

I KNEW TIME was running out for me. We had trained in Páirc Tailteann and Sean named the team back in Bellinter afterwards. No Graham Geraghty, no Darren Fay, no Mark O'Reilly – all suspended. They were going to be huge losses for us.

With Darren and Mark gone, I was the only member of the 1996 full-back line left. We were down to the bare bones, but I was fit again and had played my part against Kildare.

This would be my 11th Leinster final, and the papers had reminded everyone that I was going for my seventh Leinster medal, which would be a record for a Meath player after I had matched Peter McDermott's total of six the previous year against Dublin. I had won more than I'd lost at that point, but still the defeats niggled away. Missing Mick in the Leinster finals in 1984 and '89, Mickey McQuillan's unfortunate fumble in another Leinster final in 1994, and the embarrassment of a 10-point hammering in '95. Another painful Leinster final loss to our greatest of neighbours.

If this was to be the end, here was my chance to go out on a high and make a little bit of history. I knew time was running out for me.

AFTER WE WON the All-Ireland in 1996, I played throughout the league that winter and into '97. I felt good. I only missed one game against Kildare. I was never one for taking a break, but that league of all leagues, I couldn't have even if I wanted to – eight of the lads were suspended after the melee against Mayo! Pat Spillane might have had a laugh about it on *The Sunday Game*, comparing Jimmy McGuinness to Michael Flatley, but the GAA wasn't laughing and came down hard on ourselves and Mayo.

Not surprisingly, we didn't have a great league. We beat Tyrone in a play-off to stay in Division One, and I think everyone was just happy that it was over and we could look forward to the championship. Sean would always send us back to train with our clubs after the league campaign was done, and then he'd bring us back in a month or six weeks before the championship. I was starting to have problems with my back at the time – and I pulled a hamstring in training in Dalgan Park when I went back in with Meath. It was the first time I ever had hamstring trouble. We were doing that drill where you zig-zag with two other lads while hand-passing the ball over and back - the kind of thing we'd done hundreds of times. I felt this sudden pain, like someone had stuck a knife in my leg.

That was the start of my problems.

For the first round of the Leinster championship in 1997 we drew Dublin, just like we had in '91. This time though, I wouldn't be involved. I had walked away from the panel before the Leinster quarter-final against Laois in 1987, and I missed that game. Since then, I had only missed one championship game for Meath – also against Laois – in 1990, when I had a groin strain. That meant that I had started 42 of the previous 44 championship games. So it was a killer to miss a championship game of any kind, let alone one against Dublin.

ANYONE WHO HAS ever had a hamstring injury will tell you that it can take five or six weeks to come right. If we got over Dublin, I knew I'd have my work cut out to get my place back. The likelihood was that if we won that game, the team wouldn't be changed for the next day.

We did win, but only just.

We started like a train and were on top all over the field for most of the first-half. With 34 minutes gone, we were 1-10 to 0-4 up and it looked like we were going to hammer them and get some revenge for 1995. Then… BANG!

Keith Barr scored a goal.

Dublin tacked on a couple of points before half-time and we went in just four ahead, having led by nine a few minutes before. I was sitting on the bench togged out, even though I wasn't fit to play any part.

Dublin got it back to a point in the second-half, but we pulled away again and were three up going into injury time. It looked like we'd done enough, until Dublin were awarded a penalty by Brian White right at the death.

Keith Barr and Charlie Redmond had both missed penalties against us into that Canal goal in the past, but I didn't think we'd be so lucky this time. After a bit of jostling and messing around, Paul Bealin stepped up and smacked it off the crossbar. If it was an inch or two lower, there was no way Conor Martin would have got near it.

Nigel Nestor caught the rebound and the final whistle went immediately. We were blessed to get the win in the end, but we should never have been in that position given the lead we had. It was great to get over Dublin, but tough not to be involved.

It was Kildare next and by the time that game came around I was back to full health and desperately hoping I might get back in. One evening before training in the lead-up to that game, I was out at the front of my house mowing the lawn when Sean pulled into the driveway. When I saw him coming in I knew that it was either going to be good news or bad. He got out of the car and came over to me.

'We always measure ourselves against Dublin,' he reminded me, '… so I have to stick with the same team.

'I have to stick with those lads.'

He was right. Dublin had always been the yardstick for us, and I totally agreed with his decision. I was disappointed that I wasn't starting, but I took it on the chin. We had beaten Dublin and we had no injuries. Of course Sean had to go with the same team again.

Mind you, I could have killed Nigel Nestor for playing so well on his debut and catching that ball at the end!

I KNEW THEN that things were starting to turn against me – that it might be the end of the road fairly soon. It was the first time in over 10 years that I hadn't been picked when available, so it started to dawn on me that maybe my days in a Meath shirt were numbered.

Also, 1997 was the year of the three-game saga with Kildare. I didn't start the first game but I came on for Enda McManus early in the second-half of the second game. I had the leg heavily strapped, and I could still feel the hamstring pulling a little bit, but I didn't give in. I got through that, and I started the third game.

Those Kildare games were almost as intense as the Dublin games in 1991. Maybe people don't remember them as clearly now because the Dublin-Meath rivalry was traditionally bigger. If I was being honest, I would say Kildare probably could have won it on either of the first two days. In the second game, Jody Devine came on and kicked points from all over the place in extra-time. We were six points down at half-time in extra-time in that game, and we got it all back with points.

You'd never think that would happen, you'd imagine we'd have needed a goal. But Sean always told us to just keep the scoreboard ticking over.

And he said exactly that to us at half-time that day.

I'm sure everyone – fans and players alike - thought we needed a goal to get back into it, but it's amazing the effect that putting a few quick scores on the board can have. Some of the points Jody got that day were just fantastic. With every one that went over, we could see the Kildare heads dropping, the doubts starting to creep in. Our reputation for coming back was well known at that time and I think that put a bit of fear into teams.

When we got it back to three, the crowd really got behind us and started to believe we could save it. We got level, and actually went a point up, which was incredible. But Kildare levelled it right at the end.

I was always a believer in taking the points unless a goal is really on, and that's what we did that day. That was an incredible game to be involved in, and the rivalry between Meath and Kildare at that time was massive. The crowds at those games were phenomenal, too. There were over 54,000 at each of those two replays. That's for a Leinster semi-final. It's sad to look back at that and compare it to Leinster today.

The first two of those three Kildare games were definitely the toughest; the last game wasn't quite as tight as the previous two – we were a little bit ahead for a lot of it – but we suffered a few massive body-blows in those games. Graham got sent off in the second game, and Mark O'Reilly and Darren Fay got the line in the third.

In that third game, a ball came in and I broke it down. When I was bending my back to pick it up, I felt something pulling and I couldn't quite get down to it, so I just toe-poked the ball away.

It was another warning sign of what was to come.

Kildare would not have been known for their bravery – that's what was said about the Kildare fellas traditionally. But when you look at the players they had in that team, you certainly couldn't say that about them. Glenn Ryan was an outstanding centre-back. Martin Lynch could play midfield or full-forward. Brian Murphy from Cork was a handful. Davy Dalton was a tough man at full-back. Niall Buckley was an incredible talent in midfield – he could run, he could field, he could score and he was a hardy boy into the bargain. They had a lot of really good footballers. Their style of play was all hand-passing, give and go stuff, and it was hard to handle.

With Dublin we always knew what to expect from them because we played them so often, but we hadn't really played Kildare at all in the years before 1997. They were every bit as tricky as Dublin. Their only problem was that up front I always felt that they were depending on Lynch to click. If he clicked, everyone else did, too.

They had the likes of Declan Kerrigan, who was a really good player, but more of a playmaker than a scorer. I always thought that if Lynch went well, Kildare would go well. I felt that if we held him, we'd have a great chance. He was their danger man.

I was on Pádraig Graven, who was a decent free-taker, but didn't really do much from play. He wasn't going to win too many balls or take me on.

The other thing that Kildare team had was pace. They had some serious speed-merchants, and played a running game, but their finishing often let them down. They always struggled to put the ball over the bar. We got through that third Kildare game thanks to a goal from Ollie Murphy, and then we had 13 days to get ready for the Leinster final.

AROUND THAT TIME, the way it was going with me not getting my place regularly, I probably knew that Sean thought my time was coming to an end. That was what gradually got into my head after I didn't start the first day against Kildare. Even though I knew it was hard to change a winning team, I'd have been straight back in at any other time in my Meath career.

It was strange sitting on the bench and, God forgive me, hoping someone might pull up and I might get on! But as long as the team won, that was the main thing. Having been there for so long and having started so many games, to be on the bench was tough.

MAYBE SEAN SAW something in training?

Maybe I had lost a yard or two of pace?

Pulling the hamstring and having to let that recover for four or five weeks, it couldn't have happened at a worse time. To miss training just before the championship and for that length of time at my age – I was almost 34 - set me back a bit.

Sean might have thought that, too.

I got on with it because that was the only thing I could do. It was also the right thing to do. Deep down though, I was raging.

Sitting in the dugout was awful.

There's nothing you can do, and very little you can even see. You want to be out there. I can never sit still at the best of times, so I found that very hard. Someone has to be on the bench, and I consoled myself with the fact that I had had a good run at it. It made me appreciate all the lads who had been on the bench for all those years, who hardly played at all but never complained, and trained as hard as the rest of us.

Even though I'd been out of the team, I found it easy enough to slot back in when needed against Kildare. I never felt like I was out of my depth in spite of the few little niggles and pulls. I felt good apart from that.

I knew where to play and I knew what to do. Once I got back in, I started thinking like I was going to carry on doing this for the rest of my days. It was easy to think like that when I'd known no different for so long. That was how I'd always thought about it.

I should have known better. I didn't know it at the time, but I had already played my last championship game for Meath.

WE WERE THROUGH to another Leinster final, and I was looking forward to it and training hard. Getting ready. I'd played the full 70 minutes in the second replay of the semi-final, so I was back in.

Here we go again.

Another big day in Croke Park.

Preparing for Offaly.

The game was on a Saturday, so we trained on the Tuesday in Dalgan Park and Thursday in Páirc Tailteann. After training on the Thursday, we went back to Bellinter House, as always, for a bite to eat. We had a team-talk and I drove home.

There wasn't a bother on me.

Everything was fine. I was picked at corner-back, with Enda McManus at full-back and Donal Curtis in the other corner. We were weakened, but I thought we still had just about enough experience and class to get us through.

When I woke up on Friday morning, I couldn't move. I knew there was something seriously wrong, but I didn't know what. I rang Jack Finn, our team doctor for all of Sean's years in charge.

'Jack... I'm in a bit of bother here.

'I don't know what's wrong... I've a pain in my back, and hip.

'All the way down my leg.'

He asked me had I felt anything in training the night before? I said no, told him training had been fine.

'I'll call out and have a look at you!' he replied.

When he arrived, Jack examined me and gave me a few injections. That was grand, and I felt better for a while. As the day went on though, the pain started to come back again.

I wasn't in work because I had everything done by Thursday. With the game being on a Saturday, I had taken the Friday off to rest up and get myself ready. I rang Sean and told him that I was in serious trouble.

I told him that I didn't think I would be able to start. 'Say nothing for the moment,' Sean said. 'Sleep on it… see how it is in the morning.'

We met in Bellinter on the Saturday morning, and I was barely able to walk. It was killing me. I met Jack again and he gave me a few more injections.

I really thought it was a muscle injury. It was in my hip and right down my leg. However, the pain eased off a bit again and we got to Croke Park. Jack examined me again.

'I just can't… it's unbearable,' I told Sean.

That was it; there was no way I could play.

I did a bit of a warm-up, but I was barely even able to do that. I should never have togged out. It was heart-breaking to miss that game, because I knew I was really close to being finished with Meath. Not alone that, but the entire full-back line from 1996 was now gone.

I thought the lads were in hard luck to be sent off in the Kildare game. In my opinion, they were sent off in the wrong, for sweet damn all.

I would have had every faith in the fellas that came in for the Offaly game, you'd have to. Deep down though, I was dreading it a little bit. We were missing a whole line from the team, and what was probably our strongest line in '96. I'm not just saying that because I was there - you had Mark and Darren, who had come in for their first season and they had been unbelievable. We played well as a unit. I looked after them, and they looked after me. So it was a big hole to fill. I thought we'd still be good enough to beat Offaly.

But, deep down, I was worried.

I was sitting in the dugout in severe pain looking on. With the injuries and suspensions, I started to think that we were up against it. I think some of the other lads might have thought it was going to be easy, but these games rarely are. It turned out to be an absolute nightmare.

Goals killed us that day – we conceded two in the first-half.

People will probably think back to that game and say we were never in it, but having been 10 points down after 20 minutes, we got it back to five at half-time, and then to three early in the second-half.

Just when it looked like we might make another miraculous recovery, Roy Malone got a ball out near the sideline on the Cusack Stand side. He was only about 10 yards away from where I was sitting, and he just took off.

A huge gap opened up in front of him.

He must have run about 50 yards with not a hand put on him, and he buried it in the back of the net. That put them eight points up with less than 20 minutes to go, and that was the killer blow. Every time we got back in touch, Offaly were able to just keep the scores ticking over and keep us at arm's length.

That third goal really finished us. It was horrible to be sitting there watching all of that happening, believing that those goals would never have gone in if we'd had our full strength defence.

PEOPLE OFTEN TALK about the 1987 and '88 team, and say that that team should have won more All-Irelands. However, I would say the same about the 1996 team, maybe even more so.

We battled hard to win that All-Ireland in '96, and I thought there was another one there for the taking in '97. If we had won Leinster, we would have gone on to win the All-Ireland, I'm sure of it. Kerry beat Mayo in the final that year, after taking out Cavan in the semi-final. Mayo beat Offaly handy enough in their 'semi', but I'd have been confident that we would have beaten Mayo again.

That would have been a great game after what happened in 1996.

The pain I was in watching that Leinster final was incredible, and what was happening on the field wasn't helping. Once I was sitting, I wasn't too bad, but I couldn't stand up at all – it was agony.

We went upstairs to the bar in the Cusack Stand after and had a few drinks. The pain down my leg was getting more and more severe. Eventually I made my way down in the lift to the back of the Cusack, and was trying to walk out. I was really struggling to move. When the lift doors opened, who did I see but Des Cahill from RTÉ and Mick Holden – the former Dublin player, God rest him. They were on their way out. I played against Mick in the 1984 Leinster final and he gave me a belt that nearly killed me. I never forgave him for that!

I had come down in the lift with Samantha and a few others, but Des and Mick saw the shape I was in and carried me out of Croke Park and back to my car. So you can imagine how I felt having two Dubs carrying me out of there, as if the day hadn't been bad enough!

But fair play to them. The car was parked in Clonliffe College and they carried me that far. I had to forgive Mick after that.

Samantha drove me up to the Skylon Hotel and I got sitting down in a chair. I didn't move from there. I probably should have gone straight to hospital, but we were after losing so we were drowning our sorrows. The more drink I had, the worse the pain was getting – normally it would be the other way around!

I found out a short time later that I had a disc lying on a nerve. It literally happened overnight. I had trained as hard as I ever did in the run-up to that game and there wasn't a bother on me. Then, just like that, I couldn't get out of bed.

ON THE MONDAY morning after the game, I nearly crashed my van.

I went off to work, even though I knew that I probably shouldn't. Working for myself, I felt I had to go, even though I was still in huge pain. I came down Flower Hill in Navan, which is one-way now but was two-way then. When I got to the traffic lights, I couldn't get my leg up to put my foot on the brake.

I got an awful fright. Thankfully, I managed to hit the brake just in time, but I came straight home and lay on the floor in pain. I was brought into Navan Hospital that evening.

They did x-rays and put some weight on the end of my leg to ease the pain. I was put on medication, but I wasn't getting any better. Colm O'Rourke came to see me. He told me that his brother, Ciarán was a surgeon in Mount Carmel Hospital, and that I should go to see him. I went to see him and he gave me more medication. 'Take that for a month. If there's no improvement… we'll operate,' he informed me.

I was happy that I had a bit of time to see if the medication worked. After that, if an operation was needed, so be it. Football was obviously on my mind in terms of getting myself sorted and getting back playing, but work was a huge issue, too. I couldn't afford to be out of the van for too long. I took the medication, but once again it made no difference.

The decision was taken to operate.

I was admitted again to Mount Carmel, and Ciarán O'Rourke came around and said they were going to operate the next morning. I was really nervous, because I'd never had an operation like that before. With it being my back, which is such a delicate and difficult area, I was definitely worried. My sleep that night was restless, but I knew it had to be done; I couldn't go on with the pain any longer.

I remember going into the operating theatre and getting the injection to put me under. My mind was racing. The outcome of this operation was going to have a massive impact – not just on my working life, but also on what was left of my football career.

I had the operation in early September, and Martin Breheny from the *Irish Independent* rang me up beforehand. 'I hear you're after having a back operation? Isn't it amazing what 12 months can do… this time last year you were getting ready for an All-Ireland final!' I'm not sure if he was trying to cheer me up, or make me feel worse!

As far as the football went, there was no doubt that I was going to get back. The doctors said that I should be able to play again, no problem, once I followed the rehab program. I was never one for cutting corners so I had no problem with that. It was probably a tougher time for Samantha than for me. Jane was three, Brian was only three months old and he was in hospital in Drogheda – he was very sick with croup – and I was in hospital in Mount Carmel. So she had three babies to look after, and I was probably the biggest baby of them all!

Samantha did a lot at that time to keep everything going at home, and her parents and mine would have helped out, too. If it was me in that position, I probably would have cracked up, but Samantha is never one to panic or let things get on top of her. She just keeps going and does whatever needs to be done.

I eased back into things bit by bit.

I got out on the bike after a few weeks, then the Meath team went away for a week to Lanzarote in the New Year and Sean had me out in the sea. He was a great believer in the healing power of the salt water.

When I came back home, he had me up to my waist in the colder sea water in Bettystown. Before long, I was back running and training away again.

I MADE MY comeback for St Michael's in February of 1998 in a league game against Rathkenny. We won, I kicked two points and my brother, Robbie saved a penalty late on, so it was a good day all round for the family. We played Dunderry, too, and I felt no ill-effects from the injury and soon had my confidence back.

I started to think I'd get my place back on the Meath team, sooner or later.

I rang Sean and he told me to come back in and do a bit with the squad. We were training in Páirc Tailteann and Dalgan at the time. Then Sean was taking the lads up to the Hill of Tara, but he said he didn't want me going up there after having the operation on my back. He told me that they'd be up there for three or four weeks, and that he'd contact me when they came back down.

I was busy training with my club and doing extra stuff on my own, so I kept myself right while I was waiting for the lads to finish up in Tara. The weeks passed, but no call came from Sean.

Maybe that was his way of letting me down gently. Sean never liked confrontation and would never have told anyone that he didn't want them.

I rang him again and asked him what the story was? Did he want me back in, or not?

'Oh yeah… come back in,' he said.

So, I went back in.

I played a few challenge matches and thought I was doing okay.

We beat Offaly, 3-10 to 0-7, in the first round of the Leinster, which was great in one sense as it was revenge for 1997, but on the other hand, it just made it all the more sickening that we had been missing so many for that game.

I played a couple of challenge matches during that Leinster championship campaign. We played Cork the week before the Leinster semi-final against Louth, and then Tipperary ahead of the Leinster final. I was marking Declan Browne in that second game, which was no easy task, and he kicked a few points off me in the second-half.

I was almost trying too hard in those games. I felt like I was being looked at more than most, so I was putting myself under pressure and thinking that I needed to do things differently, or go a bit harder. It's hard to explain.

If I made a mistake, it was playing on my mind more than it would have done in the past. Sean never put me under pressure, but I was putting myself under pressure. In my mind, if I made a big mistake, I was going to be gone.

We met Kildare in the Leinster final, and lost out to a late goal from Brian Murphy. Darren Fay and Donal Curtis both went for the same ball under the Nally Stand and Murphy hung back, and stuck it in the net when it came across. Conor Martin nearly got to it, but it just went under him.

Lights out.

Our second Leinster final defeat in-a-row, and our fourth in five years.

I thought I should have got a chance that day, but so did every other lad on the bench, I'm sure. I didn't complain about not getting on, that's something I would never have done. You leave it to the manager and selectors to decide, and that's something I'd say to young lads now. If you bide your time, you'll get your chance to prove people wrong in the end.

That might have been as good a time as any to call it a day.

But, I wanted to finish on the field of play.

I didn't want my Meath career to end in the dugout.

I STILL TOOK a long look around me when I was leaving the field that day, because I realised it might be my last time in Croke Park as a player. I didn't get on, we'd been beaten... I knew that was probably it.

It was on my mind that the next time I'm here, I could be waving to the crowd at half-time in an All-Ireland final, amongst a long line of older and long retired Meath footballers. As it turned out, that indeed was the last time I stepped out onto the field as a Meath player in Croke Park.

I played a few challenge matches before the league started in the winter of 1998, and I thought I was going along well. We played Louth in Lordship, and we had a couple of other games. The league came around and I went training on the Thursday night before the first game against Clare.

I said to Samantha that if I wasn't picked for that game, I was going to call it a day. It felt like an age since I'd started a competitive game for Meath.

The team was named in the dressing-room in Páirc Tailteann.

I wasn't on it.

What annoyed me was there were a few lads who hadn't played any challenge matches and who hadn't trained a huge amount, and they came straight into the team.

After Sean named the team, I looked at him and he looked at me. I cut him in two with a glare. Neither of us said anything, but he would have known how angry I was. We went back to the Ardboyne Hotel for some food after.

I met Sean on the way out.

I was still fuming and I sat him down.

'I think it's time for me to pack it in,' I told him.

'If I can't get my place for a league match, and with lads coming back and getting in ahead of me... there's not much point in me hanging around.

'I feel I'm being hard done by, and I don't think you'll need me.'

I can't remember what Sean said back to me. It was something like... 'You're one of the best players I ever had... I'll be sad to see you go.'

I think he also told me... 'If that's how you feel, then so be it.'

And, that was that.

We shook hands and parted ways.

When I told Sean I was quitting, I was really hoping he'd ask me to stay.

I was disappointed that he didn't reply... 'Look, we still need you... stay on for another while.'

In hindsight, when he mentioned the Hill of Tara and told me to sit it out, maybe that was his way of telling me he didn't want me. Maybe it would have been better if he had told me it was over, and presented me with the brutal truth. Maybe if he had taken me aside and said... 'Look, thanks for everything Martin, but we won't be needing you anymore.'

That would have been easier in some ways.

IT WASN'T EASY for me to deal with my decision. I was convinced if that injury hadn't happened to me in 1997, I would have played for Meath for a couple more years.

I would say that maybe Sean had been thinking about how serious my injury was, and he didn't want to see that happening again. Whatever it was, he had his reasons. We didn't speak for a few months, but that was it.

There was no big showdown or shouting match, but I was gutted. It took me a few years to get over it.

It felt like a death in the family. I took it really badly. Between minor, under-21 and senior, I had been a part of it and it had been a part of me for over 20 years. Now, all of a sudden, it was gone.

Sin é.

The fact that I wasn't a Meath footballer anymore was hard to get my head around. It was a part of my identity. Other lads could probably have walked away and it wouldn't have cost them a thought. Bob O'Malley said he never missed it once he left.

I wish I could say the same.

I came home that night after leaving the Ardboyne Hotel and I was like a child of 10 in the kitchen with Samantha. I cried my eyes out.

The routine was gone, and there was a massive hole left in every week. I used to love training. So, when I'd come home on a Tuesday night after work, all the panic and rushing around was over. There was no getting the gear ready, heading out to Dalgan or Páirc Tailteann. That all stopped.

No more trying on the new gear the night before a big game, no more Garda escorts into Croke Park.

No more summer evenings training out on the field in front of hundreds of Meath fans.

I had been doing this for 20 years, and all of a sudden it was gone.

Nowhere to go, nothing to do.

I found it hard to fill in the time, and I'd say I was tough to live with around that same period of time. But the kids were young, so I was able to spend more time with them. Samantha was very supportive when I was playing, because she knew what it meant to me. Jane was born in 1994 and I hadn't really been around that much for her, so it was nice to have more time to spend with the kids and help Samantha, which I probably didn't do as much as I should have when I was playing.

In the winter, it was easy not to miss it. But when the championship rolled around, when the weather picked up and the ground was hard and all you wanted to be doing was training with the lads – that's when it hit home.

It was torture knowing that I could be out there or, in my mind at least, I should be out there. Still, in the back of my mind, I was hoping I might get the call back in.

I was playing well with the club.

Maybe I'll get one more shot.

THE FIRST GAME I watched after I parted ways with Sean and the Meath team took me back 11 years to 1987, when I walked away from it all for the first time.

It was tough looking at it.

Once again, like '87, Meath were playing Laois.

Once again, I was watching from the stand.

This time, however, I wouldn't be coming back. There would be no phone call from Sean. What was done was done.

CHAPTER 1

200,000 IN NEGRO MARCH

"About 200,000 marchers, negro and white, paraded through Washington yesterday in a mass call to the United States Congress to bar racial discrimination in all aspects of American life. President Kennedy conferred for 75 minutes with 10 leaders of the organisations which sponsored the freedom march. In a statement later, the U.S. President said that the cause of 20,000,000 negroes, seeking to secure equal treatment for all, had been advanced."

MORE MONEY FOR PHONE DEVELOPMENT

"The Government had decided to make available the funds required for telephone development and it had become possible to tackle the development of the system on a realistic basis, the Minister for Posts and Telegraphs, Mr. Hilliard, announced in Navan. Two factors that made a noticeable impact on the phone services this year were the succession of storms and blizzards and the visit of President Kennedy."

The Irish Independent

MARIE AND PADDY are my parents.

I think everyone knows Paddy! They were very much involved in football. My mother came from a big footballing family, the Dillons in Syddan. For as long as there has been football in Syddan, there have been Dillons representing the club.

My father would always have been into football. He's originally from Carlanstown, but his father is from a place called Rathsharkin up in Antrim, beside Ballymena, and he came down to Meath to manage a farm. Of course, he ended up staying in Meath because he met his wife and had a family here. My father still has family up north who are very much into the GAA. Some cousins of mine play with the Antrim footballers and hurlers, so the GAA has always been in the family, going way back.

My father was a coalman. We weren't wealthy, but we weren't deprived of anything. Nor did we get whatever we wanted all the time either. There were four of us playing football, and we had one pair of boots between us. The fact that there was a bit of an age gap helped with the sharing of those boots.

I remember the first game of football I played underage. I got the boots and I'd say I wore six pairs of socks to fill them. That was an under-12 or under-14 game. They were Blackthorn boots. I never had boots of my own for a long time, but it wasn't something I thought about because it was the norm. When you got to adult, obviously everyone had to have a pair of boots then. But at underage level, where we could all share the same pair, then that's what we did.

THERE'S EIGHT OF us in the family. I've three sisters and four brothers. When we were back at home, it was football from morning until night. We lived in a small bungalow, and every Sunday there could have been 20 young fellas in the back garden from 11 o'clock in the morning til 10 o'clock at night.

We'd play 'Three goals and in'.

Then we'd play 'Three points and in'.

We'd be going all day long. My mother used to call us for dinner and sometimes we wouldn't even go in. It was just football, football... football, even at that age. I always think back on those days with great fondness. We had nothing to worry about, only kicking a ball around in the back garden.

My father worked hard at the coal, but during the summer it wouldn't be that busy, so he needed to find something else to do to keep the money coming into the house. He'd get into a tractor and mow hay for the farmers around the area. That was him – the coal lorry in the winter and the tractor and hay in the summer. My mother was always at home, she never worked outside the home. She was always at home rearing the whole lot of us, so that kept her busy. I'm sure there were days when she wished she could get away from us and go out to work!

I went to the local primary school, Carlanstown National School. I liked it there and I was always well-mannered in class. Now, I wouldn't say I was the brightest spark, but I always behaved myself. The teachers at the time were very much involved in football, and I probably concentrated too much on football and not enough on my homework, but I liked school all the same. Like most schools at that time, especially rural ones, we only had three classrooms. I think there were only 10 boys and 10 girls in my class, maybe less.

After I finished primary, I went to 'The Tech' in Kells. I left there when I was 15, which I should never have done, but that's just the way it was at the time – we all had to go out and work and bring home a few quid. A lot of lads around that time did the same. There wasn't nearly as many people going on to Third Level back then. It was the norm for lads to drop out of school after the Inter Cert, or Junior Cert as it's now known.

Jimmy Gaffney was my best friend in secondary school. He was a really good footballer, and played in goals. He was brought in for a few trials with the Meath minors when he got to that age. Maybe I just got a lucky break, I was picked out.

Most of the lads in my class played football, but I was probably the only one who progressed. We all know people like Jimmy, though. Up and down the country there are fellas with stories like that. We can all name lads whom we played with in school or underage or wherever who were very talented, but who just drifted away from football or sport for whatever reason.

I'm not sure, exactly, what the difference is between lads who progress and those who don't. I suppose there are a lot of different reasons why people give up on Gaelic football or hurling or whatever sport they have a talent for. They probably don't think too much about why they don't give it their all, and I never thought too much about why I always did. It was just something that was in me from an early age. That's not a criticism of anyone who makes a choice one way or the other. Everyone is different and everyone follows the path that suits them.

There I was anyway, Inter Cert done, and not a clue what I wanted to do with myself after that – other than play football. That wasn't going to pay many bills. I was never afraid of hard work, however, so I went off and ended up trying out a clatter of different jobs.

While I was still in 'The Tech', I used to milk cows in the morning before

I went to school. I had a motorbike – a little Honda 50 – and I would get up really early in the morning. Daddy would be gone with the coal lorry, and I'd get up and do the milking and feed the calves on a farm down the road. I'd then come back and get changed, hop back on the motorbike, ride it into school, and I'd be back working on the farm again after the last class.

So I was really putting work ahead of my schooling. I was putting everything ahead of schooling when I think back on it.

MY MOTHER WOULD probably have been happier if I had stayed in school. Daddy was more inclined to think I should be out working and making a few quid. If you ask young lads of 15 nowadays what they want to do, nine out of 10 of them could tell you.

I have to say, I had no idea what I wanted to do.

None whatsoever. Maybe if I had stayed on and done my Leaving Cert, it might have become clearer, but at the point in time when I left school, I really had no idea what I was going to do or where I was going to end up. That probably explains why it took me a little bit of time to find my groove and why I walked away from a few jobs that I didn't think suited me. That would be something which would apply to my football career, also.

My first job was as a joiner in a place in Kells. A brother of mine was a carpenter, and he told me that this place was looking for an apprentice, so I said I'd chance it. I think I was only 15 or 16. I hated it, absolutely hated it. It was inside, and it was dusty and warm. I knew very quickly that it wasn't for me.

I used to have to ride a bike into work and ride it home… a push-bike! I had a motorbike going to school, and a push-bike when I was going to work, so that'll tell you how things were going for me at that time! It was about six miles in and six miles home. It was just so dusty, then I had to work on a Saturday when there was a lot of sport on the television, and I was missing out on that. In the end, I just gave it up. I couldn't stick it any longer. It only lasted about two or three months in total.

So, that was joinery scratched off the list. I still might not have known what I wanted to do, but at least I knew there was one thing I definitely *didn't* want to do.

Next up, I saw an ad in *The Meath Chronicle* for an apprentice mechanic in Tara Motors on the Kells Road, just outside Navan. I applied for that and got the job, in spite of not having the first clue about cars or engines. A second cousin of mine was working there at the time, so I got a lift in and out with him. I had no training, but you learned on the job. A mechanic would be over with me, he'd show me how to do a full service – this is where the oil goes and so on.

I didn't like that job much either.

I was up early in the morning, getting a lift in with my cousin, not getting home until late – you wouldn't know what time you'd get home. The cousin was fond of a few drinks aswell, so he might stop off on the way home and I'd have to walk the rest of the way. It wasn't great. So, again, I gave that up after a fairly short period of time. Thinking back on it now, there were lads who would have been only desperate to get a job, and here was I after walking away from two in the space of a few months.

My parents must have been wondering how many jobs I was going to give up on, but I think that the main problem with the joinery and the mechanic's job was that I just didn't like being inside. I was after being out and about all my life up until then.

Out the back playing football, out working on the farm.

I just couldn't get to grips with being stuck inside all the time.

The building was next. Finally, a job I liked. I worked with three builders from Dulane – Mickey, John and Danny Reilly. I was only a labourer, but I was outside, so that was a good start straight away. It was an early start and the work was tough enough – I used to mix the cement and carry it up to the three boys – but I enjoyed it. The money was good, too, unbelievably good for that time really. This was around 1980.

I was a young lad with money in my pocket, but I couldn't really spend it. I used to give my mother a few quid each week and she'd put it away for me. In fairness to my mother and father, they never took any money off me; I just gave it to her and said, 'Mind that', and I'd hope to God she still had some of it! I didn't move out of the family house until I was married at 28… I got a lump sum then, minus the interest! Twenty punts in the 1980s would do someone a long time, and that's all I'd have in my pocket. Well, maybe a little bit more just in case. I didn't really go out a lot, because I was in with the Meath minors at the time. I really had no interest in going out.

Work and football was what I was keen on – I wanted to make the Meath minor team, and I wanted to progress on and on football-wise. That was really it for me at that time. I trained Saturdays and Sundays, and the football probably kept me on the straight and narrow, which was a good thing. Also, I had a few extra pound in my pocket that I never had at the joinery or as a mechanic.

I WAS OUT in the fresh air.

I worked Monday to Friday, and had Saturday off – but I could do a bit on a Saturday if I really wanted to. It was great.

Then one Friday evening, Mickey Reilly came over to me.

'Martin…we're finished!'

The building had been going really well at that time, but all of a sudden there was some bit of a crash in the economy. BANG… the job was gone.

I had been doing it for about 12 months, the longest stint I had ever done in one job. I was really loving it, and it kept me right, kept me fit. I was never going to be anything other than a labourer, because the lads were never going to show me much more than that, I felt, but I was attending the three of them so I was up and down ladders with buckets of cement which was tough going. There were no lifts or anything like that!

To finish up in the building was a bit of a shock. It was a Friday evening that I found out I'd no work – just like that. I had received my wages and had hopped into the car to go home. Another good week done. Next thing was, I got a tap on the window. It was Mickey.

'That's us finished… we won't be here anymore, Martin.

'We'll have to let you go!'

That was it. I went home and told my mother and father. Soon enough, I was back helping my father out on the coal lorry, but I knew that I had to get something else fairly quickly, because my father wasn't able to pay me as much as I'd been getting. I had to get some money for myself.

About two weeks later, I saw an advert in the *Chronicle* for an apprentice butcher with Sam Black in Navan.

'Look… I think I'll chance this,' I told my father.

Now, no disrespect to Sam, but the money was completely different to what I'd been getting for working on the buildings. It was probably less than half of what I was on, so that was a good kick up the backside after having been on the kind of money that you nearly couldn't spend it – a lot of people would say that I wouldn't spend it anyway! But it took a bit of getting used to. When I started working at the butchering, there was no more handing money to my mother. What I got had to do me.

That was just the way it was though. I wasn't one to sit around feeling sorry for myself. I just had to get out there and get another job. I was lucky that I seemed to be able to pick up work relatively easily.

I don't remember what was involved in the interview, maybe boning a bit of meat or something, but it was very easy to get used to, compared to the mechanical or joinery work. I was inside again obviously, but it was different. The only thing I said when I started at the butchery was that I could never kill.

There was a slaughterhouse, but I never went near it. I was an animal lover, so I hated killing. But, back in the shop, I was shown the ropes and away I went. I picked it up quickly enough.

I was in at nine o'clock and worked until six. I had to work Saturdays, but I was off on Mondays. There was no Sunday opening back then, so that meant that I had Sunday and Monday to myself and for football. In fairness to Sam, at the time I would have been on the minors or the under-21s, so he would give me time off to go and train. It was never a hassle. Any time I needed off, I got.

Sam was very fair to me. So maybe he and the lads I worked with had a lot to do with why I enjoyed it. Sam and the lads were all big GAA men. Sometimes if you're working with lads who aren't into the GAA and you're getting more time off than they are, people can give out. That didn't happen once.

The whole crew were all footballers, and we all helped each other out. As well as that, the interaction with customers was something I had in the butcher's shop that I didn't have in the other jobs. There were always great characters who would come into the shop, and we had great banter.

As the years went by, everyone came to know me, and people would be coming in and wanting to talk about football.

There would be a lot of football to talk about.

CHAPTER 2

MONDAY, JULY 27, 1981

FASTS COULD GO ON ALL YEAR

"The hunger strike deaths in the Maze Prison could continue until the end of this year, with the number of deaths reaching double figures, a member of the National H-Blocks/Armagh Committee said at a rally outside the GPO in Dublin on Saturday, before the march to Government buildings. Mr. Jim Gibney, who is also a member of Provisional Sinn Féin, told the crowd that the prisoners in the H-Blocks must be given the support they were entitled to. 'They will end their hunger strike only when the British Government concedes their five demands,' he said."

DUBLIN SIDE LESS THAN IMPRESSIVE

Dublin 1-8 Meath 0-9

"Dublin regained the Leinster minor football title after surviving great pressure applied by a determined Meath team towards the end of a disappointing match, in which scores were at a premium at Croke Park yesterday. The truth of the matter is that if Dublin had managed to translate all the chances that came their way in the first-half, Meath would not have been in a position to seriously challenge for the title in those closing minutes. Just as they were poised to punish all of Dublin's first-half shortcomings, Meath were suddenly themselves struck by a similar squander bug and, had they taken their chances, Martin O'Connell's late point could have been the winner for them."

The Irish Times

FROM A YOUNG age I think I had a natural ability for football. When you come home from school and you get a ball and you're straight out into the back garden, that has to help. There was nothing else for me at that time, only football. I had no other distractions. Maybe if I had, things mightn't have turned out the way they did for me.

I always believed that I was good enough. That might sound like arrogance, but it was nothing like that. I wasn't cocky, but I had huge belief in my own ability, and I always thought that if I was given a chance, I'd have a right go at it.

Mattie Kerrigan was over the Meath minors at the time I was coming through, which was good for me. Mattie had seen me play a few times underage, so I would have been on his radar. I was mad to play for the minors. I just wanted to pull on that green and gold jersey.

So I was called in for trials. Back then, there were no mobile phones or WhatsApp messages, so someone in the club would have received word from the county board that they wanted me to come in so they could have a look at me. My mother, or Paddy McIntyre used to bring me. Sometimes the club chairman at the time, Jim McCormack, would drive me. You'd have been grateful to people for things like that.

Everyone from the club wanted to see me doing well, so they would make sure someone was around to take me to trials. I went to maybe three or four, so obviously the selectors must have seen something, or so I thought. After the final trial, I knew they'd be picking a panel of lads soon enough. I was fairly sure that I was going to be selected.

But I was actually dropped off the panel, for some reason. It was a big shock to me. It definitely gave me something to think about.

Not long after that, I was playing for St Michael's against Skryne in the quarter-final of the Junior championship. Before that game, my father had gone into Kells and he bought me the first pair of boots that I could call my own. They were Blackthorns, black and white. I can still see them to this day.

I was delighted with myself, and it was a brilliant thing for him to do. It probably seems like nothing now, but I was thrilled to get them. I went out to play that game and I felt great, purely because I had these new boots on me. I was playing right half-back.

I went out onto the field – remember, this was a couple of weeks after I'd been let go from the minor panel – and I was thinking to myself… *I'm going to prove these fellas wrong. I'm going to play well tonight.*

It was a Friday night in Páirc Tailteann, and I gave an exhibition. I couldn't do anything wrong. I played out of my skin. Two days later, Mattie Kerrigan rang the house to ask me to come back into the minor panel. That's where it all started.

Like plenty of Meath seniors, before and since, I never played under-14 or under-16 for the county. We used to play against some of the Meath underage players in club games, and they could never get a kick of a ball off me. My father would always ask aloud… 'How can Martin not get onto the Meath under-14 panel… when he's playing against these lads and doing better than them?'

He might not have been the most impartial judge, but he believed in me, and I suppose he was proved right in the long-run.

DESPITE THE FACT that I had confidence in myself, I dreaded going out against those fellas, but I'd build myself up. *These lads are on the Meath team… I'm gonna show them I'm as good… or better than them,* I'd tell myself.

So, I just got it into my head that those lads wouldn't get the better of me. I was usually playing centre-back or midfield at the time. Wherever I played, they couldn't handle me. That's not being cocky, that was just how it was. So I knew I was good enough, it was just a matter of getting a chance.

When it came to the minors, I felt hard done by to be left off the panel, but that drove me on even more to prove that I was right and they were wrong. Luckily enough, that's the way it turned out, and that Skryne game set the ball rolling to get onto the Meath minors. My father was a driving force.

'Go out and prove those lads wrong,' he'd tell me. Even when I got onto the Meath senior team, he'd always be pushing me to do well. He was very driven, so maybe that's where I got my drive from. But that night in Navan against Skryne, he really drilled it into me to go out and prove Mattie and the selectors wrong.

It was rare at the time for a team from north Meath to be playing in Navan – or 'The Showgrounds' as many people would still call Páirc Tailteann - so it was a big deal for me and I wanted to do well.

It was the shop window, if you want to call it that. Of course, the flipside was that if I'd had a bad game, I definitely wasn't going to get called in. But I was so determined to play football for Meath, so I had to perform. I wanted to be the best. That's just how I was, there's no other way to explain it. I wanted to be the best I always wanted to play for Meath, always wanted to win an All-Ireland, always wanted to win an All Star, always wanted to get to the highest level I could playing football. That was what drove me. My father would have been the same; my mother would have been a bit quieter. My brothers would have been every bit as good as I was, but I just got the chance and I took it. So the call came from Mattie.

'Will you come back in?'

Back in I went. That was the start of 16 years in a Meath jersey.

I was delighted to be back in there. At that time, we used to train in Páirc Tailteann. The way things were back then – and this'll show you how things have changed – the minors used to train in one half of the field, and the seniors were in the other half. I remember one evening, there could have been 25 or 30 of us training at one end with the minors, and I looked down to the other end.

I counted 14 seniors training.

14!

THE MEATH SENIORS were at a really low ebb at that time. The county hadn't won a Leinster title since 1970, and had endured a really dismal spell since then. Dublin had beaten them comfortably in the 1980 Leinster semifinal, Wexford knocked them out in the quarter-final in 1981, and they lost a preliminary round game to Longford in '82, so things weren't going well at senior level. The county's last Leinster final appearance at that time had come in 1977.

So, to see a handful of lads out training that evening in 1981 told its own story. It was no surprise that they were performing so badly in Leinster.

We trained twice a week, and then on a Saturday or Sunday. It won't surprise people to hear that there was nothing too scientific about it. We just ran. A lot. Then we ran some more, did some sprinting and played a bit of ball. Shooting drills, tackling drills – nothing too fancy. When the games came around, there wasn't really much in the way of tactics, and there were definitely no dieticians or stats people. It was catch-and-kick, every man for himself. There was no set pattern of play; everybody just had to be better than their direct opponent and that was how you got across the line.

That Meath minor team had Donal Smyth in goals. Colm Coyle was there, Bob O'Malley, too – I think he played three years at minor. Coyle was minor the previous year, also. I played right half-back on that team. We got to a Leinster final that year against Dublin in Croke Park, but we were beaten by two points.

Even at that stage, you could pick out the lads who would go on to have senior careers, if they stuck at it. You would have picked out Coyle and O'Malley a mile off. Bob's game never changed, even when he went up to senior. He always played from the front, never panicked, and always had loads of time on the ball. Anyone who knew anything about football would have picked him out.

I would have played in Croke Park once or twice before that Leinster final. At that time, we were in the old dressing-rooms – I mean the really old ones – under the Cusack Stand. I'll always remember running out and seeing the stands. It was nerve-racking. I would always be nervous, but it brought the best out of me.

I loved playing in Croke Park.

I loved the big stage, and the challenge of performing well. I'd say to myself… *If you can play well here… you can play well anywhere.*

Mattie Kerrigan deserves a lot of credit for instilling that attitude in me. He had it drilled into us. He was, and still is, a legend in Meath from his playing days and he was also very shrewd on the line. He was a great talker and had a knack for getting lads into the right frame of mind.

While I'd be nervous going out into big games in Croke Park, once I settled down, it was like any other game. Well, most of the time anyway! That Leinster minor final was disappointing. I kicked a couple of points, one was from a free, but we couldn't quite get over the line. Dublin just pipped us. I remember thinking that we left it behind us a bit. We had chances but didn't take them.

After forcing my way onto the minor panel, and then onto the team, my next focus was on playing under-21 for Meath. Unfortunately, that didn't go to plan. I was injured for two of the years that I was eligible. I broke a bone in my ankle for one, and broke my collarbone another year. I only played one under-21 championship game for Meath. That was against Dublin in Parnell

Park in 1983, and we lost. I was selected at centre-forward for that game.

The Meath Chronicle's match report from that 1-6 to 0-8 defeat was kind to me. "Martin O'Connell tried his heart out on the forty, but doesn't seem suited to this position." It would not be the last time that the question of my positioning raised its head.

AT CLUB LEVEL at that time things were going along fairly well. I won a Division Three championship in 1978 with Carlanstown – that was the inaugural year of that competition. We beat Rathmolyon in the final after a replay. At that time, there were two clubs in the parish – Carlanstown and Kilbeg. I remember they played each other a few years before in the league. I was only a young fella, so I wasn't playing, but I was watching on from outside the fence. There were 'killings' in that game. It was horrible to see lads from the same parish doing that to each other. Little did they know then that they'd be playing alongside one another soon enough.

Kilbeg were going nowhere at that time, and a lot of the Carlanstown lads who had won the Division Three championship in 1978 had stopped playing. So, in 1980, the decision was made to amalgamate the two teams into one. There was really no other option but to join up. All you'd ever have had were two bad teams. Both clubs would barely have won a game, never mind a championship. In spite of the previous rows on the field, once we joined, there was no trouble at all. A lot of these lads played underage and in school together, so they knew each other well.

The name of the new club was St Michael's, and we got off to a good start. We reached the Junior A championship final in 1981, but lost after a replay. In 1982, we went one better. We played Seneschalstown in that year's final, and we were odds-on favourites. We got out of jail in a big way, got very lucky, but won by two points. I played alright – I was well able to run, so I covered a lot of ground. I started at centre-forward, then I was moved to centre-back, so I was in and out of the game. It definitely wasn't my best game, but we got over the line. I liked playing centre-back, but we had a very good centre-back at the time in Jackie Lynch, so they had to put me somewhere else at times.

The reason I liked playing centre-back or wing-back was because I was facing forward, facing the ball. My whole career I was happiest facing the ball.

We went up to Intermediate in 1983 and we were beaten in the semi-final. After that, we lost a few players who stepped away. We didn't win an Intermediate title until 1989, so that was a long time to wait. One thing I always thought was that a lot of lads gave it up a little bit too early. Some might say I didn't give it up early enough! Maybe the amalgamation had something to do with it, I don't know. That was their decision, but they gave it up too early in my eyes. There were a few more years left in a lot of those lads. Having said that, we had success. Given the way things were before the amalgamation, it was great that it turned out so well and that we achieved something together on the field almost immediately. That wouldn't have happened if there was any in-fighting going on.

IN THE QUARTER-FINAL of that Junior championship in 1982 we played Dunboyne in Navan, and we won handy enough. I had a good game, and kicked a few points.

I was marking an older guy who was playing corner-back and I gave him a bit of a roasting. Maybe he made a mental note of that.

His name was Sean Boylan.

CHAPTER 3

HIGH CRIME RATE IN MEATH-LOUTH

"The number of armed robberies carried out in Meath and Louth last year was for the second consecutive year the highest in the State, next to the Dublin Metropolitan area, according to the Garda Crime Report for 1981. The report shows that the Louth-Meath division has the fourth highest crime rate and the second lowest rate of detection of indictable offences."

BOYLAN THE NEW COACH

"Sean Boylan (Dunboyne) is the new coach of the Meath senior football team following the withdrawal of the outgoing occupant of the position, Mick O'Brien. Boylan, the only nominee willing to accept the post, said at last Monday night's meeting that it was an honour for him to take the job. He is a former coach to the county hurling team and more recently had been acting as masseur to the senior football side.

Boylan said that a lot of hard work lay ahead, but added that he was not afraid of hard work. He remarked that he would be prepared to accept criticism but would be prepared to accept help too, and asked for the co-operation of the clubs.

Colm O'Rourke said that the coach and selectors would need to get full co-operation from the county board and was critical of the fixing of midweek club games shortly before important county games. O'Rourke called for greater emphasis on the county team, adding that goodwill from all was needed. He promised that the coach and selectors would get the support of the players if they get it from everyone else."

The Meath Chronicle

THERE'S AN OLD story that still gets told today, that when people heard Sean Boylan had been appointed Meath manager, they assumed it was for the hurling team.

He was a hurling man as everyone knows, but he was the only one who wanted the job of managing the footballers back in 1982. Things had not being going well, so it wasn't a prestigious role to take on. Over time, thanks to Sean, and the men on the sideline with him, and the squads he assembled, the prestige would return in a way that didn't seem possible back then.

Not long after he got the job, Sean contacted me and asked me to come into the senior panel. I was going well with my club at the time, but I was a bit surprised to be brought in at that stage, as I was still only 19. I would have to bide my time before getting my chance, though.

I still remember our first meeting with Sean so clearly. He took us into the meeting room under the stand in Páirc Tailteann. There might have been 30 lads there. Sean introduced himself, told us what he was about, and what he was going to do to try to get this Meath team up and running. He got the respect of everyone in that room – both the older lads, and the new, younger fellas. I was very impressed.

I was sitting beside Colm Coyle and Bob O'Malley because we all knew each other, but I was looking around the room at the likes of Colm O'Rourke, Gerry McEntee, Mick Lyons and Joe Cassells. They had been there since 1975 and had been through the mill, but won nothing. So they were ready for someone to take this thing on, and you could tell that they straight away liked what they were seeing and hearing. Sean got respect from everyone, you could hear a pin drop that night.

He just had that aura about him. Whenever he came into a meeting with us, the first thing he'd do would be to take his watch off, and he'd put it down on the table, and there'd be complete silence from that moment on. He did that right the way down through the years.

When you saw the watch coming off, you knew he immediately had the attention of the entire room. He just had that control.

When we were all walking out afterwards, there were a few lads who were saying… 'Sure he's a hurling man… what the hell is he going to know about football?', but they didn't say that to his face. Nothing was said in the room, everyone held their peace. There was a bit said afterwards alright.

Lads were hedging their bets. They didn't want to be kicked off the panel before they'd even started!

Sean brought a huge amount of professionalism to the whole set-up. His training methods were ahead of their time. Everything was done on time - he had footballs out, bibs out, and we got grub after training. So it was all done for us, which wasn't the case in 1980 or '81, I believe. He was very structured, very well organised. There was no waiting around, it was just go, go… go in training.

As well as all that, Sean had a great way about him. He could talk to the younger lads, the older lads… he could get inside our heads very quickly. Now there were times later on when many of us felt like choking him, but that never happened. You might feel like doing it, but you'd never actually do it!

SEAN SET THE tone from day one.

He made it clear that there would be a lot of hard work involved, and a lot of pain and suffering. But if we all bought into it, we'd get the rewards. We used to train in Páirc Tailteann, we used to go out to Dalgan Park – the home of the Columban Fathers four miles outside of the town – and we used to go up to the Hill of Tara. Winter or summer, we might be told to assemble on the beach in Bettystown. So, you never knew what was coming next, training was never the same.

There was always something different. He brought great professionalism into it. He had a great team around him. Mochie Regan was the masseur, Mick McAuley – 'The Crow' we called him – was there, too. He had a great backroom team, they were just a barrel of laughs those lads, great characters. You need that on the field and off it, and Sean had them all over the place. He was just different. I don't know what the previous management was like, and I never trained under anybody but Sean Boylan for Meath, but he was brilliant.

WHILE IT WAS great being in with the seniors, the training was a big shock to the system for me. It was a serious step up. There were a lot of very, very tough sessions. There was a lot of running, a lot of sprinting, and a lot of tackling.

Even though the training I had done with Mattie Kerrigan and the minors was tough, and the club training was tough, this was just… way up there.

Another level entirely.

We'd do laps of Páirc Tailteann, we'd run up and down the hills behind the goals, we'd hang off the crush barriers on the terrace and bang our stomachs against them... mad stuff. We'd all be asking each other, 'Why do we need this for football?', but it was strengthening our core. There are different ways of doing it now, of course, but that was the old fashioned way – laying over the barrier for maybe 10 seconds – hands out and legs out, just hanging there.

Sean wanted us to do chin-ups.

In the tunnel under the stand, there was a little gap in the cement where we could get our hands into a space and take a grip, and there we'd be, up and down... up and down. Two lads at a time, 20 pull-ups. Then another two fellas came in.

He had us running up and down the steps of the stand, and those steps are no joke. It's mad stuff when you look back on it now, but it's still being done in certain places. What we maybe didn't appreciate at the time was the mental aspect of it. We were pushing ourselves so hard. The lads who had been around for a few years were driving it on and the younger lads wanted to impress the older guys and make their mark, so everyone was giving it one hundred percent. Nobody wanted to be seen to give in or look weak, so that really helped us develop the mental toughness that people would soon see in Meath teams in the years to come.

When the games came around, I had to wait my turn. It was the back-end of the league in 1982-83 before I got a run. The league was played at the end one year and the beginning of the next at that time. But I was only 19, and the training was so enjoyable even though it was tough. I knew there were big names ahead of me and that I just had to bide my time, so that's what I did. It didn't bother me.

That being said, you can only do that for so long – hanging around on the verge – so I pushed myself hard at training to get onto the team. Sean had a word in my ear now and again.

'Your chance will come,' he promised me.

'When it does... make sure you take it.'

I'm not sure how I got my first start. I was probably playing well with the club and going well in training. I got onto the team, and I grabbed my chance with both hands. But I knew myself that, the way I was playing, it was only going to be a matter of time. Sean explained that to the likes of me and

Coyler. He said it to a lot of the younger lads.

The older lads? They knew they were going to be on the team. There was 'The Big Four' – Mick Lyons, Gerry McEntee, Joe Cassells and Colm O'Rourke. I remember someone saying to me… 'You'd think this was a boy band!'

Those four lads were cemented in the team, even though Sean gave Mick Lyons a jolt at the very beginning by dropping him for the early rounds of the league. I had looked up to them for so long before I was on the panel. So, when I went in there myself, I felt under a lot of pressure to prove myself to them above everyone else – to prove that I was good enough to be in there.

I hugely respect Mick, Colm, Gerry and Joe to this day. If Mick Lyons rang me up tomorrow and said, 'Martin, I want you to do something for me,' I would jump to it, and the same with a lot of the other lads. With some others, maybe you'd have to think about it!

Having Mick Lyons, especially, in defence with me helped me to settle quickly into the scheme of things. Mick was great for giving advice to all of the backs. He'd point out the things you were doing right, and also things you were doing wrong. He would give you a bollicking if it was needed, no doubt about that! There were countless times in a game he'd let me know if I did something wrong. The same in training.

It might come to blows at times – and that did happen – but it was never unhealthy. We were all striving to get things right, for everyone's sake. There were occasions when a few of the forwards might be annoying Mick, and Mick would take lumps out of them, which was no harm! But he was great. If I ever needed a bit of advice, I'd go to Mick.

Now, if you played against the same lads in club football, they'd probably lift you out of it, but that was to be expected.

THERE WAS A theory going around at the time that the Meath senior team wasn't performing well because the rivalry was so intense at club level. Supporters believed that lads couldn't put that to one side when they played for the county.

I never got any sense of that. If there was any element of it there at the beginning, Sean sorted it out and knitted everything together fairly quickly.

If you were playing against one of the Meath lads for your club, you'd nearly try to avoid each other. I remember playing Summerhill in Navan one year. I was midfield for St Michael's and Mick was midfield for Summerhill. We stayed on opposite sides of the pitch for most of the game.

But with some of the big senior clubs, like Navan O'Mahonys, Skryne and Summerhill, there would have been a huge rivalry and enmity, built up over decades. Joe Cassells and Mick got stuck into one another in a club game one year, but Sean had a few words with them after that. He always said to us to be careful when we were playing with our clubs. What he meant was, don't get injured. Don't get stuck into each other and get sent off or do something stupid. It did not always work out like that. Club football and the pride of the parish will always spike.

In 1989, Mick Lyons broke his leg in a Feis Cup semi-final against Gaeil Colmcille. He went for a ball with his usual fearlessness and came off second best. That's what Sean meant about being careful when playing club football - he didn't want lads picking up serious injuries. Of course, it was very difficult to go out and not give one hundred percent, and that was the kind of player Mick was – he was full-blooded in training and in games. No matter what jersey he was wearing. The green and gold of Meath, or the blue and yellow of Summerhill.

THINGS STARTED TO turn around under Sean.

We got a bit of success in 1983 when we won the O'Byrne Cup. I was starting to play a few games and getting a taste of it. We met Longford in the final, and I was picked at centre-back. I learned a lesson that afternoon that stayed with me for the rest of my career.

The night before that game, there was a function on – a Meath Butchers Association dance in Athboy. Being young and naïve, I didn't forget about the game exactly, but I decided to go to the function and have a few drinks – which turned into a few too many. The next morning I was in a bad way. I think I fell asleep on the way down to Longford for the game in Pearse Park.

I started the game and I didn't even make it to half-time before Sean took me off. "The selectors experimented by placing young Martin O'Connell at centre half-back, but the St Michael's player lacked the experience for such a demanding role, and was switched with Pádraig Finnerty in the 23rd minute and taken off just before the interval," *The Meath Chronicle* reported on May 14, 1983.

I can't remember the game at all, but I know I was terrible.

I was in no state to play. It was my own fault, and it was the first and last time I ever drank before a game. I'd preach to young fellas now to never do that, but I did it. We all have to learn the hard way, I suppose. Thankfully, we won narrowly, 1-11 to 1-9. We were lucky enough. Colm O'Rourke kicked four points, and Mickey Downes from O'Mahony's got the goal. Mickey was also the captain and lifted the trophy afterwards. It was only the O'Byrne Cup, but it was silverware, so that was a huge thing for us.

Sean came over to me the next night at training. He asked me was I out the night before the game? I had to tell him the truth.

It was a lesson learned not to go drinking and acting the eejit before playing a game of football. Sean, in fairness to him, came to me first. He always found things out. I didn't think he would, but he did! He spoke to me first, and then he spoke about what had happened to the lads in the dressing-room. And rightly so. He could tell from the way I looked and played. Maybe he was testing me out and seeing if I would own up or tell him a blatant lie.

The warning I got from Sean scared me straight, and it was the last one of those I got, too. Looking back on it now, I was a young lad, just out of minor and straight onto the senior panel. I probably didn't realise how serious it all was – but something like that incident makes you realise very quickly that it is *serious*. That O'Byrne Cup victory got the ball rolling for the Meath team, and for me, even if the final was one to forget from my perspective.

CHAPTER 4

MONDAY, JULY 4, 1983

AFTER WINNING THE O'Byrne Cup we were confident going into the championship. The draw pitted us against Dublin in the Leinster quarter-final. Not for the last time, we took them to a replay. We really should have won that game the first day, but missed a lot of chances, and Dublin got two fairly fortunate goals.

Barney Rock scored with a lob from 35 yards, then Phil Smith deflected the ball into his own net. We felt very unlucky that day. In the replay, Mickey Downes had a penalty saved by John O'Leary, so we didn't get a whole pile of luck in either of those games. Dublin went on to win the All-Ireland that year – in the infamous final against Galway when 12 Dubs battled against 14 men from the west – so we knew that if we could take them to a replay, then we were moving in the right direction. I didn't play in either of those games, I was still serving my time on the bench.

The following year, 1984, marked 100 years of the GAA.

A competition to mark the occasion was organised by Croke Park. It was called the Centenary Cup, and had an open draw, straight knockout format. It was played in April and May of that year, before the championship started. We played Carlow in the first round, Laois in the second round and Galway in the quarter-final. We beat Galway 2-18 to 0-11 in that game in Tullamore. With Galway having been in the All-Ireland final the year before, beating them so comfortably was another little boost, even if it wasn't a championship game.

We played Cavan in Croke Park in the semi-final. A lot of teams really wanted to win that competition, because there would never be another Centenary Cup, not in our lifetime anyway. We were on a bit of a roll at that stage. We didn't normally have competitive games so close to the championship, so we looked on all of this as a bonus and something to make the most of.

In that semi-final, Cavan started at a serious pace and should have had two goals in the first five minutes. If they took either of those chances, it might have been different. As it was, we settled down and ended up winning easily in the end. I played in the half-back line. At last, I was beginning to establish myself on the team.

Next up was Monaghan in the final, and that felt like a big deal for us at the time. Playing in a national final was something I hadn't experienced before, and there was a crowd of over 30,000 in Croke Park that day, which would have been the biggest crowd I'd ever played in front of at that point.

I don't remember that game being a classic by any means. We were level at half-time, but in the second-half we edged clear, and won by two points (0-10 0-8). It was a massive achievement for us to win something, given that Meath hadn't won anything in so long. Now we had the O'Byrne and Centenary Cups in successive years. It felt like winning an All-Ireland at that stage. After the game, we were brought to a reception in Ballsbridge. Ford had sponsored the competition, so they had laid on a bit of a do. The two teams met and we had a bit of dinner and a few drinks and a chat, and then we headed home.

That was it. We were back training the following Tuesday.

Nobody went mad.

PEOPLE OFTEN ASK if I could imagine, at that time, the kind of success that lay just around the corner. What I thought at that stage was, once we got into that winning habit, we could beat anyone on our day. I felt that the mixture of the young lads and the older lads was really bringing things on. Everyone felt that Meath were on the up.

The spirit that we had – did that come from winning, or did we win because we had that spirit? It's hard to say. I could definitely feel the growing bond among the lads.

Sean instilled that into us, too, that spirit. Whatever team you play on, you can always sense when there's a good vibe in the dressing-room, and when everyone is putting in the work and pulling in the same direction. That's how it felt in the Meath team at the time. We knew that something special might be possible.

While all of the players and Sean felt that, he never said it outright. I'm sure he knew, but he never let us get ahead of ourselves. We kept our feet on the ground and took one game at a time. Sean knew that he had a good group. But there was still rebuilding work to be done. A lot of the guys from the Centenary Cup winning squad were coming to the end in their county careers. The likes of Mickey Downes, Ben Tansey – God rest him – Gerry McLoughlin… they were on their way out, and I don't mean that in a bad way. They'd given great service to Meath. Young lads were taking their places, like O'Malley, myself, and Coyler.

I finally made my championship debut in 1984.

We played Westmeath in Mullingar and I was picked at left half-back. We won easily, which was another sign that things were going in the right direction, but I remember that game for two different reasons. First of all, I played really well – *The Meath Chronicle* called me "Majestic O'Connell" the following week, which was a huge thing for me to see at that time.

Martin Breheny, in his match report for the *Irish Press*, agreed. "For the fourth time in seven weeks, Meath have won an important game by 13 points. The Centenary Cup champions flashed a warning to the rest of the football world that they are on the move for the Leinster title. Man of the Match Martin O'Connell ran himself into near-exhaustion to ensure Meath confirmed their superiority and, with the task achieved, he was withdrawn."

More good reading for me. On the downside was the other thing I remember most from that afternoon – with about 10 minutes to go, I got a bad injury. I went down to pick up a ball and one of the Westmeath lads kicked through my fingers and snapped two bones in the back of my hand. That was me out for six weeks. After waiting for so long and getting my chance, this happens. I tried to play on, but the pain was too much.

Aside from that, it was a great performance from us on a scorching hot day in Mullingar. I was marking a fella called Eamonn Coughlan, and all the lads had me believing that it was the runner! With me only being a young fella and knowing no better, I thought... *Jesus, maybe it is him!* The injury kept me out of the Leinster quarter-final against Louth.

We got over Louth without playing especially well, then I was back in for the semi-final against Laois, who gave us a real fright. We were three points down with 15 minutes to go, but Colm O'Rourke got a goal which turned things in our favour, and Ben Tansey got another one late on to make the result safe. Maybe all of the games that year had taken a bit of a toll on us. I know some of the reporters were saying that winning the Centenary Cup and then going straight into a Leinster campaign might have been the reason we weren't playing that well – especially against Louth – but we had made it through to a Leinster final, so things were still on track.

Dublin, the reigning All-Ireland champions, were waiting for us. We would soon find out we weren't quite ready to make the step up to the next level.

IN THE LEAD-UP to that Leinster final Sean drilled it into us not to have any fear of Dublin just because they were champions. We trained the day before the game. Sean told every man on the team what his job was. He told us what to expect, and what to do, but at that time there were no tactics really. There wasn't a lot to football – and I don't mean that in a critical way. It was straight-up man-on-man.

You got it and kicked it inside as quickly as you could. Some of the balls going in wouldn't exactly be pin-point accurate onto a lad's chest, but every man was expected to go for every ball. Mick Lyons and Gerry Mc, just like Sean, always said to the forwards, 'Lads... you want the perfect ball in, but no matter what way it comes in in the first 15 minutes... you better go for it.'

What they meant was, as a defender in a game like a Leinster final, you'd be lucky to get a kick of it. It was frantic. As a half-back, I could get a ball and there could be two lads coming at me. So I just got rid of it. If I had time to pick out a pass, then great, but most of the time I just had to clear the lines any way I could. In fairness to the forwards, whatever way the ball went in, they went for it. They were after being told, so they didn't have much choice!

Colm O'Rourke was the target man for an awful long time for us, especially in the years before the likes of Brian Stafford and Bernard Flynn came in. In the following years, Flynn was a player who'd live off O'Rourke. Colm would catch it and lay it off to Flynn, but I think we relied too much on Colm O'Rourke in '84 and those early years.

No matter how many lads were around him, we'd send it into him. That was the way football was in those days, though.

It was my first Leinster senior final, and there were over 56,000 people watching, which was a record for a Leinster final at the time. I remember coming out and hearing the roar... it was a big shock. I'd played in Croke Park before, but this was different. I had never played in front of a crowd that size. It was a bit overwhelming really – you might nearly get lost in the game at times. It definitely took a while to get used to that and especially to the sight and sound of Hill 16. As if the occasion and the crowd wasn't enough to deal with, I faced the daunting task of marking Barney Rock.

Barney was fairly hot at the time, a household name. I did fairly well on him that day, I think. My father always said that if I kept my man from scoring, then I must have done something right, but it was hard to keep Barney scoreless!

He got 1-4 on me that day – a goal and a point from play. I was a bit nervous, but I thought I played relatively well. We didn't get much luck on the day. Both of Dublin's goals came from rebounds after Jimmy Fay had made great saves.

We started the game fairly well, and early on we were awarded a penalty. Pádraig Lyons stepped up – but he put it wide. It was almost the perfect shot, but it nearly killed the umpire! Had that gone in, it might have been different. In spite of losing, getting to a Leinster final was huge. Maybe on the day, nerves got to us and we were overawed by Dublin being All-Ireland champions, and with Hill 16 and all that. The other thing worth noting about that game was that Mick Lyons was absent. He was nursing a broken thumb, and was a huge loss. Overall though, it had been a good year.

We'd made the National league semi-final, won the Centenary Cup, and a lot of us had our first experience of a Leinster final and all that went with it. We were building nicely, and there was a feeling that 1985 would be our breakthrough year. As often happens, things don't always go as planned, and '85 proved to be a giant kick up the backside for all of us.

Perhaps it was a turning point as well.

WE BEGAN THE 1985 championship with a win over Kildare in Navan. I didn't start that day, as Aidan Crickley was picked at half-back, but I was brought into the game. It was a fairly comfortable win and we were in decent enough shape going into the Leinster semi-final against Laois – or so we thought.

That game proved to be a complete nightmare.

We were fixed to play in Tullamore, and I was right half-back. Maybe we took them for granted. Things had been going fairly well, we'd gotten to the 1984 Leinster final and probably had one eye on another crack at Dublin. Maybe a bit of cockiness crept in. If that was the case, Laois fairly knocked it out of us.

We were hammered – beaten by 10 points. At half-time we were behind by three, but still well in it. Then, early in the second-half, Laois got two goals in a minute and we never recovered. That loss was the end of the road for a few lads on that team. To be brutally honest about it, the whole lot of us could have gone, because nobody played well. But the likes of Aidan Crickley, Frank O'Sullivan, JJ McCormack... I think that game was probably the end for them. We were beaten out the gate.

There was no back door.

Everything had been going in the one direction until then – upwards – then all of a sudden there was a whack, and it was a new experience. We always felt that we would beat Laois, whether we played brilliantly or not. It would always be tough for sure, but we'd generally come out on top. We were in the old dressing-rooms in Tullamore, and had to walk out through the crowd and onto the field.

After the game, there was just complete silence. The defeat sickened us after the high in 1983 winning the O'Byrne Cup, and the Centenary Cup win in '84 and getting to a Leinster final.

We thought that 1985 was going to be a big year. It didn't happen. Sean said a few words, then that was that. Everyone thinks Sean is quiet, but inside those four walls he was often a different animal. He would read the riot act if we weren't performing or if we were not putting it in. We walked out of the dressing-room, and spent the next six months back with our clubs. It was a big bump in the road that none of us saw coming.

CHAPTER 5

WINNING SONG

"Ireland's representative for this year's Eurovision Song Contest in Norway is the five-piece band, Love Bug, who emerged clear winners of the National Song Contest finals in RTÉ last night. With 35 votes, they topped the voting with Kevin Sheerin's song 'You Can Count On Me'. Dazed and overwhelmed with their win, the group was nevertheless disappointed they were not allowed to phone their families in Co. Down from the station, and eventually had to reverse the charges from a public phone box."

DUBLIN ROCK STEADY

Dublin 2-8 Meath 1-10

"This National Football League quarter-final at Croke Park yesterday will be remembered more for the dourness rather than the brilliance of the exchanges. It was a game outsiders Meath might have stolen, but which Dublin probably deserved to win because of their better discipline plus their facility for snatching telling scores against the run of play. Meath once again proved that they can never be written off. They served warning that they will be a championship force if they can tighten up in certain areas and cut out elementary mistakes."

The Irish Press

WE TOOK THE league very seriously, because we hadn't won a huge amount at that stage, and it was another title to aim for. Sean generally brought us back about a month before it started. With the league played either side of Christmas at that time, counties had four games before the break. So, if you won three of them, you were in good shape for the second part of the campaign. We had a decent run of results and qualified for a quarter-final with Dublin. We lost, but we ran them close again so we weren't too disappointed. It felt like we were really close to getting the better of them. Patience!

We went into the Leinster championship with belief that we could, finally, make the breakthrough. Our first game was against Carlow in Dr. Cullen Park. We didn't play well but we got through it. I was picked at half-forward again, which I wasn't too happy about, and I was replaced by Liam Smith. In the semi-final we got by Wicklow easily enough but I didn't start. I came on for Gerry Mc at half-time.

It was frustrating not to be able to get my place given that a couple of years before, after my debut against Westmeath, it looked like I was going to be a regular from then on.

But, we were back in the Leinster final again.

It really felt like we were ready this time. We'd had a taste of it in 1984 so we knew what to expect, then got the kick up the backside against Laois in '85. Once again, I was left out of the starting 15 for the game. I have to be honest, I really took the hump at not starting.

It turned into one of the wettest, most miserable days you could imagine. David Beggy was new into the team that year. That game was his first time to ever play in Croke Park, and only his second time to even be in the place – the first was a U2 concert! He got a ball early on, took off with it, slipped a couple of times, but got up and kicked it over the bar. That set things going, then the heavens opened.

It was a really scrappy, dour game given the conditions. We got across the line by a couple of points (0-9 to 0-7). The low-scoring tells you what kind of a game it was. I came on with about 15 minutes to go - in the forwards – and didn't do particularly well. I was just told to go in and help the lads out. I might only have touched the ball once or twice. Maybe Sean was hoping for a repeat of the game when he marked me and I kicked a few points, but that didn't happen!

It was absolutely spilling, so it was the worst day you could get to come on as a sub. I was dreading it because it was such a hard game to get into. We were definitely the better team on the day, maybe the more determined, too. O'Rourke kicked a couple of points, and Finian Murtagh had a really good game that day. Liam Harnan ran into Barney Rock in the run-up to half-time. It was a serious collision. Barney dislocated his shoulder and had to go off, which did our chances no harm. I don't think there was any malice in it, the two of them just slipped into each other going for a ball.

Not starting took some of the good out of it for me, but the celebrations were every bit as good as if I'd been on from the start. It was the biggest thing I'd won up to that point, and to beat Dublin – because we hadn't beaten Dublin in anything for decades – was huge. That was our first Leinster title in 16 years. We went back to the Ashbourne House Hotel for some food and a few drinks, and the main street in the village was packed – that was really when it hit me. We'd been training and playing away and in our own little bubble to an extent.

Beating Dublin in a Leinster final instantly elevated us several levels, and it gave our hungry supporters something to latch onto and to really celebrate. Seeing the public outpouring of appreciation for us was great. It told us that a whole county believed in us. In fact, the whole county was now in the same bubble as the team itself!

That was when things started to change, and people started to recognise all the players. I probably thought I was a great lad for a while, but then you start copping onto yourself. No matter where we went, we were known. I thought that it was going to be like that every year, that we were going beat Dublin every time we played them.

We had an All-Ireland semi-final ahead of us, and we had Kerry staring right back at us. We were about to enter a whole new ball game. Me? I ended up back in the starting team, but in the last jersey I expected to have on my back.

SOON AFTER THE Leinster final, we played a challenge match to open a pitch in Kilmainhamwood. PJ Gillic – who I've never forgiven to this day! – went off on his holidays after the Leinster final, and not just for one week.

PJ went for three!

Off he went, and we were opening this pitch a couple of weeks before we were due to play Kerry. We met Cavan, and I was picked at full-forward. It was probably the worst thing that could ever have happened to me, but that evening I couldn't miss with any ball that came my way. I scored six points off Damien Sheridan.

Now, no disrespect to Damien, but I was going to be coming up against tougher opposition in a couple of weeks' time. So all the talk then was of me playing at full-forward against Kerry. Lo and behold, that's exactly what happened.

I was happy to be starting, but we had a team talk before that game, and I was more confused coming out of it than I was going in. Some lads were telling me to do one thing, Sean was telling me to do another – and a few other fellas were telling me something else! I was walking with Liam Hayes to our cars, when he turned to me.

'Well… what do you think?' he asked me.

I did not know what to reply for a second. Then, I admitted, 'I haven't a clue what I have to do!'

Sean was telling me not to come out beyond the 21 yard line, and to move right and left and pull my man out of position. Then Liam and Gerry were telling me to come out a bit further, so in the end I kind of did my own thing.

Not surprisingly, I got one kick of the ball in that game.

One kick, one point, so a one hundred percent record!

It just didn't work out for me or the team that day. We were going really well until Kerry got a bit of a break. Joe Cassells, Mick Lyons and Mickey McQuillan all went for the one ball and collided really badly. Ger Power was waiting and tapped the ball into an empty net. There was another moment later in the game when we'd got a few scores and had the crowd behind us and, all of a sudden, Tommy Doyle went down injured, which totally broke our momentum.

There was a bit of cuteness there from the old Kerry heads who'd won all those All-Irelands. That was an ageing Kerry team though, and I thought going up to Croke Park that day that we'd have a great chance with all the young lads we had. But that bit of experience from the likes of Tommy, Jack O'Shea and Pat Spillane made the difference.

We were probably a little bit daunted by the prospect of playing against some of those same household names. I was marking Seánie Walsh, who was a legend. Deep down, in all honesty, I think we thought we had enough done by winning Leinster. We probably celebrated a little bit too much. You could say that was our All-Ireland that year.

We might not have taken the semi-final seriously enough. We felt confident that we could beat them, but it wasn't the end of the world if we didn't. Losing that game wasn't as sickening a feeling as some other games we lost. Like, PJ going away would never have happened any other year. So we probably didn't put football first for that Kerry game. In fairness, PJ probably had the holiday booked from way back. He probably didn't expect to win a Leinster title! But I think we were happy with a Leinster and if we won the semi-final, sure that was a bonus. We'd learn quickly enough that that's not the way you should look at these things.

Ger Power's goal and Tommy Doyle lying down were the big incidents I remember from that game. We were on a bit of a roll at different stages, and Bernard Flynn was giving Páidí a few problems, but we were well-beaten in the end. Wille Maher got a goal late on, and in the build-up to that Mick Lyons tried to hit Ogie Moran a shoulder and missed him, and ended pole-axing Liam Hayes instead.

But that was Mick, if he didn't get one of the opposition, there was a danger he could hit one of his own!

A FEW YEARS later, Seánie Walsh was asked who was the worst player he ever played on in Croke Park?

He said, 'Martin O'Connell'.

I met him maybe 10 years later, and I gave him a little bit of stick over it! In fairness to him, he admitted he was one hundred percent wrong, and sure I was playing out of position! But Seánie was a huge name at that time, he could play at full-back or midfield. It was a little bit intimidating even shaking hands with him before the ball was thrown up.

THE INTRODUCTION OF a few new faces in 1986 was great for the squad. Beggy used to come to training on a motorbike, he was a great character to have around. A few things started falling into lads' laps due to football, too. Brian Stafford had a company car, Flynn had a job with Tennent's, so a few lads started arriving to training in fancy cars. Things were coming the way of lads that wouldn't have if the football wasn't there.

Beggy and Flynn were great characters. I took it very seriously, whether I was training or playing a match. But everyone is different. Harnan was very witty, and Flynn was liable to do anything or say anything – he still is! There was a great mixture, but overall, we were all very committed and took it seriously. Training was tough, and we took even bigger lumps out of one another.

It was a case of, 'May the best man win!'

There was an element of pressure on lads who were new to the panel. They were tested out in double-quick time. But it was always a little bit like that, and when I first came in, you'd have lads trying to get a clatter at you to see how you took it. You had to earn the respect of the men who were there. As much as we were a team and a panel, every lad in there was pushing hard for a spot, so if a new face came in, you would be sure he'd have to prove his worth. Not only in terms of his football ability, but also – and maybe more importantly – in his physical and mental toughness.

Even in the latter years of my career, I remember Cormac Murphy joined the panel and one evening he was up the other end of the field in training, shouting and roaring like he'd been there for years. Harnan came over to me.

'Who the fuck is that?' he asked me.

He didn't wait around for an answer.

'If he comes down here, he added, '… I'll shut him up for a while!'

And that was just the way it was. Besides, if Sean thought a new lad was weak, he'd be gone. Good luck. Baby-sitting was not on the agenda.

CHAPTER 6

THE LAST HURRAH

"That perennial soccer chorus, 'We shall not be moved' never carried more meaning than at Milltown yesterday when Shamrock Rovers supporters protested over the club's proposed move to Tolka Park. About 200 of the fans invaded the pitch at half-time in the FAI Cup semi-final clash with Sligo Rovers, which may have been the Hoops' last ever match at the ground, their home for 50-odd years."

GALWAY TOO GOOD FOR WEAK MEATH
Galway 1-8 Meath 0-9

"After wintering in the barren wastelands of Division Three, Galway's footballers gate-crashed their way back into the elite club in yesterday's league quarter-final at Portlaoise. Chaotic Meath were generous contributors to the Galway Rehabilitation Fund as they ruined themselves with one of those insecure displays that has tended to haunt them in recent years."

The Irish Press

I WAS GETTING impatient. I had been on the panel for three or four years, but still hadn't nailed down a regular starting place.

On the odd occasion when I did start, it wasn't in my best position at left half-back. I played there in 1984, but then there was a change of selectors. There were five selectors, including Sean, in his first few years as manager, but then there were only three – Sean, Pat Reynolds and Tony Brennan. Whether one of them took a dislike to me, I don't know, but I was playing everywhere but left half-back for some reason.

WE WENT INTO the 1986-87 league with plans to have a good crack at it, because we really wanted to keep the momentum going and take it into the championship. We had a good Division One campaign. Páirc Tailteann was being renovated at the time, so we gave up home advantage for our opening game against Dublin. It was no big deal because the way we looked at it, the more games we got in Croke Park, the better.

I kicked a point after about 20 seconds of that game, I remember that much! I was playing at wing-forward again and we won the game easily. It was another important marker laid down by us, because we knew that, barring a miracle, we would be meeting Dublin in the Leinster final in 1987. We had another landmark win against Kerry in Kells just before the Christmas break, but I didn't get on the pitch that day.

I remained in and out of the team during that league, starting one week, a sub the next. I was getting increasingly frustrated. I felt like I had served my time and when I was played in what I believed was my best position, I was doing well.

But, for whatever reason, I wasn't getting the No.7 shirt.

We ended up finishing second in Division One behind Kerry, which qualified us for a quarter-final against Galway in Portlaoise. I remember going down to that game – I had been picked at wing-forward, again – and I felt like I was getting near breaking point. I wasn't thrilled to be playing there, but I said I'd give it my best shot – try to help the team and see what happens.

I was going well enough in the first-half, or so I thought. Then at half-time I was told I was coming off. I'm not sure why. As soon as I heard I was being substituted, I said to myself... *I'm done here'*.

I watched the second-half from the bench.

'Why were you taken off,' Mick Lyons asked me, when we sat down beside one another back in the dressing-room after the game. 'What happened?'

'I don't know, Mick... but I'm out of here after this'.

'I wouldn't blame you,' he replied.

That was it, I left.

I didn't get any explanation as to why I was replaced. I assume they thought I wasn't going too well, but I thought I was and some of the lads thought I was. Maybe there was a dislike for me among the new selection team, I don't know to this day. But that was that, I had had enough of it at that stage.

I walked.

I THOUGHT IT was the right thing to do, but as time went on I started to think that maybe I shouldn't have done it. It's funny how quickly you can regret a decision that seemed one hundred percent right at the time.

I really missed not being in there with the lads. I couldn't very well pick up the phone to Sean either, though maybe in time I would have. I was hoping I might get a call to come back, and luckily enough I did. When I left, I didn't say anything to Sean or the selectors. I just didn't appear at training.

I started to believe that I should have stayed on and proved them wrong. The opening game in Leinster that year was against Laois, and I was sitting up in the stand watching on, and that's when it really hurt. I wouldn't have been a great man for watching games if I was out injured, so to be watching on because of my own decision to walk away was tough. But I did what I felt was right at the time because I didn't think I was getting a fair crack. I'd made my bed.

As always with games against Laois, there wasn't much in it, but we just about scraped through. They got a couple of goals which gave us a fright, but a few frees from Brian Stafford settled us again and we got over the line. Shortly after that game, I got a phone call from Sean asking me would I go back in? I had been away for the best part of two months at that stage.

I was still playing well with the club, so I was very glad that Sean made contact. I was back in for the Kildare game in the Leinster semi-final. I was picked at corner-forward, because Colm got a knock against Laois and hadn't recovered.

A few months before, I probably would have said, 'What the hell am I doing here at corner-forward?' but, to be honest, I was so relieved to be back in that I just decided that it didn't matter where I was playing. It was good to have a Meath jersey on again and I was going to give it my best shot. Towards the end of that game, Frank Foley got injured and I played the last 10 or 15 minutes at wing-back.

And that was it, I never looked back after that.

GIVEN THE BOND that existed within the Meath squad at that time, my walking away didn't go down too well. When I returned, I got a fairly frosty reception.

A lot of the lads didn't talk to me for a long time after I came back in. Gerry McEntee didn't forgive me until 1988, so I went a full year with Gerry! He just didn't get on with me at all. These days, we get on the best, but it took a year for Gerry to really speak to me properly again.

To this day, the lads slag me a bit about it. But I just say to them, 'Look lads... only for I came back, we'd have won nothing!' That shuts them up!

When I was back training on the first night back, the reception was cool, to put it mildly – especially from Gerry. It took until after the All-Ireland final replay in 1988 for Gerry to forgive me. He came over to me after that game and said he was sorry for not speaking to me, and that he was proud of me for the performance I put in that day. The rest of them forgave me a bit quicker, but that was the way Gerry was and I wouldn't hold anything against him for that. I was glad we made up.

AS EXPECTED, DUBLIN were our opponents in the 1987 Leinster final. At long last, I was back in the team at half-back, and I was delighted to get my chance after everything that happened. I definitely regretted walking away, but I was back in now so I was happy to put all of that behind me and drive on. That game was played on a really windy day, and the pitch was in an awful state because there had been a U2 concert on there not long before.

Being back in my favourite position was great, but I felt under a bit of pressure after having the falling out, walking away, being brought back... and now here I was playing where I wanted to play. So the pressure was really on me. I had to perform, because if I didn't, then who was right and who was wrong?

I felt a lot of focus on me, but maybe that was no harm. I was more comfortable back there in the half-back line than anywhere else. I was marking Barney Rock again, and he was a class act as everyone knows, but I was happy enough with how I played.

As the years went by, the rivalry built up dramatically between ourselves and Dublin, and so did the tension. It wasn't uncommon for there to be a melee of one form or another. Midway through the first-half, there was a bit of a dust-up under the Hogan Stand. Mick Lyons came out for a ball, and I always say to this day that if Mick had gone down to pick it up properly, he would have been killed, because Kieran Duff and Charlie Redmond were both coming in like trains.

However, Mick stepped over the ball and he nailed one of the Dublin players, I'm not sure who. I'd forgive him for that, because he would have been stone-dead if he hadn't. Then a bit of a hullabaloo started. Kevin Foley hit someone, and the referee ended up sending him and Redmond off.

But, I'll never forget, when the sending-offs happened, Redmond took it on the chin and walked straight across the pitch to the dugouts on the Cusack Stand side. Kevin being Kevin, he walked off on the Hogan Stand side, went around by the Nally Stand and past the Hill – and they gave him dogs' abuse! – and the whole way back around to the dugout.

That was the same day as Stephen Roche won the Tour de France, and I'm nearly sure the start of the game was delayed by three or four minutes because the race was nearly at an end and Roche was winning it. Just before the ball was thrown in, it was announced over the PA system that Roche had won the Tour. I don't think it was as windy in France as it was in Dublin, because there was a gale blowing down the field. Back then, with it being 'catch and kick', the ball could go 100 yards. It might go to the opposition, but it would be out of danger very quickly. But that game was my first game in my favourite position in three years. I wasn't complaining.

It wasn't the best performance that Meath team ever gave, but those matches with Dublin were always a bit of a grind, and with the weather conditions and the state of the pitch, it was just a game to win any way we could. Mattie McCabe popped up with a real poacher's goal in the first-half – he just pulled on a loose ball – and that was vital as we won by four in the end.

PEOPLE SOMETIMES ASK me if there was a Dublin opponent I didn't like marking? To be honest, I never really feared anyone in those Dublin games. More often than not, it would be Barney Rock or Charlie Redmond I would be picking up. They were tough to mark, and I respected them hugely, but I never feared them.

It was just a name, and you had to go out and do your best. Whoever it was, you knew if they were right-footed or left-footed, we knew their form, and they knew the same about us. In terms of my own game, I would say that speed was probably the one thing I lacked. I had to work a lot on my speed, I'd do extra training, extra sprinting. So speed was one thing I might have struggled to deal with, and I didn't like a lot of space in front of me.

I always like playing alongside my man or a fraction behind him. The last thing I wanted was to get turned. I hated being caught two or three yards in front, then have to chase back, because I wouldn't have the speed to chase a man down, and all of a sudden there's an extra man and maybe a goal chance.

I was always fairly tight to my man, and I'd always get a hand in somewhere along the line. As a defender, I always thought my first job was to defend. If the opportunity arose to go up the field, then I'd go. And I was a good carrier of the ball, I could solo on my left or my right, though my passing was patchy at best, and a lot of the Meath forwards would vouch for that! But that's just the way I was. I enjoyed attacking when I could, I got a few scores and set up a few scores, and I was a good fielder, but I probably could have done with an extra yard or two of pace.

After we won that Leinster final, and did the two in-a-row, I had a real pep in my step. I felt among the lads again – other than with Gerry, of course! I felt like I had proved myself in my best position and I could finally put all the drama of the previous couple of months behind me. I helped the lads, they helped me, and I felt six feet six inches tall after that game. It was a big relief, because if that game hadn't gone well for me personally or for the team, then maybe people would have been asking me why I had left, or worse, why had I bothered coming back?

THERE ARE LADS that I get on better with now than I did when I was playing with them, but as a unit, back then, everyone rowed in the same direction. Whatever happened in training or in the dressing-room stayed in there, and nobody would have known what was going on. After that Leinster final in '87, we celebrated on the Sunday night, and then it was back training on the Tuesday. We would never, ever meet on a Monday. The only time we did was in 1995 when we were beaten by 10 points.

I remember after the '86 Leinster final, we were all back in the Ashbourne House Hotel and we were like superstars, it was incredible, and we were loving it. We were all sitting around, four or five of us. Colm O'Rourke had opened his sports shop in Navan and had a few pound at the time, or at least that's how we saw it, and he gave David Beggy 50 quid to go up and buy a round of drinks for the four or five of us who were at the table.

Beggy went to the bar with Colm's money. Ten or 15 minutes went by and there was no sign of Beggy coming back, or the drinks. Eventually, he comes back down with the pints, puts them down on the table, and hands Colm two pounds in change.

O'Rourke wanted to know where his 50 quid was gone. Turned out that Beggy was after buying everyone at the bar a drink with Colm's money, and not only was he after spending it all, but he was the one getting all the credit. Everyone was saying what a great fella Beggy was buying everyone a drink.

FROM THE MOMENT we lost that semi-final against Kerry in 1986, we were really focused on going one better in '87. There was no settling for a Leinster title this time around. Our semi-final opponents were Derry, who had beaten Armagh in the Ulster final.

That game turned out to be a fairly comfortable win for us. We were fairly confident going into it. Derry had a superstar at the time in Dermot McNicholl, but he wasn't fully fit and had a big bandage on his leg. They started off really well, but missed a couple of chances. We then got to grips with them. No disrespect to Derry, but I think when we started to get on top back then, teams used to fear us, and that helped us a lot.

I got one almighty belt off Brian McGilligan under the Cusack Stand. I was going for a ball and he was coming in, so I rode the tackle rather than getting hit full-on, and I went up in the air and I could see about six rows of the Cusack Stand as I came down and landed on my back. It was a fair belt. Anyone who remembers Brian will know he was not a fella you wanted to run into. I met him a few years after and he said he thought he'd killed me.

He came close.

Only a couple of months before, I had walked away from the Meath panel.

Now all of a sudden I was preparing for an All-Ireland final – Meath's first since 1970. I had only been there a few years, but the 'Big Four' of Colm, Joe, Mick and Gerry, were getting their just desserts after all the heartache they had suffered over the years.

Derry manager, Jim McKeever spoke to us in the dressing-room after the game and complimented us on our resilience in coming back from some disappointing defeats, adding that Derry would use us as an example and try to do the same. They would get their reward in the years to come.

For me, all of the hours of hard work in Navan, Dalgan Park, Bettystown, the Hill of Tara and beyond had finally paid off. Nothing I had encountered in my career until that point could prepare me for the build-up to an All-Ireland final.

CHAPTER 7

SATURDAY, SEPTEMBER 19, 1987

MINISTER RAPS GLASS CHIEFS OVER BIG PAY-OFFS

"The Government is furious over the Waterford Glass plan to get rid of 750 workers in the biggest redundancy deal in the history of the State. Minster for Labour, Bertie Ahern said last night that the £21m earmarked for redundancy payments could be better used for investment in developing products and maintaining jobs."

MEATH POWER SHOULD SINK CORK CHALLENGE

"Cork raised eyebrows by including ex-Kildaremen, Larry Tompkins and Shay Fahy in their team, many people forgetting that five non-natives (including, whisper it, some from Kerry) wore the Cork red in the 1952 semi-final. Meath have not created quite the same fuss in their climb to the top. It has not been without its frustrations though. Sean Boylan has toiled since 1982 and broke Dublin's stranglehold only last summer, before immaturity saw them fall to Kerry. It's 20 years since Sam Maguire last visited the county and, in an area bursting with football pride, that is an intolerable wait. The excitement of the supporters at the prospect of victory tomorrow is almost unprecedented."

The Irish Independent.

IN THE WEEKS leading up to that All-Ireland final, the hype was massive. I was living in Carlanstown at the time. Leaving the village on the morning of the game was something I still remember well. Everyone was out wishing me luck and waving goodbye – you'd think I was never going to be seen again!

Flags were up everywhere. They'd even taken the green and gold manure bags and wrapped them around the telegraph poles and tree trunks. There were cars being painted, bunting up – there was just green and gold everywhere.

I WAS STILL working in Sam Black's butchers in Navan, and I couldn't get any work done. People were coming in all day long wishing me well, while others were in looking for tickets. Thankfully, I only worked the Tuesday and Sam gave me the rest of the week off. I just had to get away from the shop because my head was fried.

I don't mean that in a bad way, because of course people meant well and only wanted to show their support, but that can mess with your mind. So, I took the few days off and I went up the fields for walks and did my own thing. Once I was out of the shop and out of Navan, I was out of the limelight. I remember Liam Harnan once telling me that the best thing about being a farmer was being out in the fields all day with nobody knowing where you are or how to find you. I envied him at times like that.

Not being in the shop made it a little bit easier to keep my feet on the ground and not get caught up in the hype. Sean was very good at keeping us focused. There was one press night, and that was the only time we could talk to the media. If someone rang me the week of the game, I wouldn't talk to them. Whatever happened on the press night, that was it.

Sean made that clear to the press lads on the night, too, and there were no more interviews after that. I still had journalists ringing me up looking for a chat, but I just told them that I wasn't able to talk. That took the pressure off a bit. It is the norm now, what with media nights and so on, but back then things were a lot more informal.

That was Sean's forward-thinking coming into play again – he made sure we were done with the media duties good and early so all we had to think about was the game and getting ourselves right for it. Of course, that didn't protect me from bumping into people at home, or people ringing the house on the morning of the game to wish me well.

We were training in Dalgan Park, and there were huge crowds turning up. Once we got over Derry, we had a month of a gap before the final. The first couple of weeks, we trained as normal. Then as the game got closer, people started turning out in massive numbers to watch us train. Coming off the field after training it was not unusual to have to make our way to the dressing-rooms through thousands of supporters. People wishing us luck, cars parked everywhere, it was just incredible. I absolutely loved it.

Those crowds watching on put a little extra spurt into me. If any of us did something good we might get a round of applause. I thought it was great, but I took it in my stride at the same time. The older lads who'd been there for so long like Mick and Gerry, they loved it too deep down, because it was what they'd been waiting for their entire career.

I was only a young fella, so I probably looked at it differently than they did. They were older, and they might have thought they'd never see a day like this. I was thinking the opposite – that this was going to be a regular thing.

We got all of the potential distractions out of the way as early as possible. The press stuff, getting suits measured, gear bags, togs, socks – whatever we were getting was all taken care of well in advance. So the last week or 10 days were all about the game itself, the opposition and what we were going to do. We watched videos, and I'm sure Cork were doing the same. We analysed what every fella did, what foot to keep them on, where the kick-outs were going, who the danger men were, and so on.

The team was named on the Thursday night after training. We met on the Saturday evening in Dalgan Park. We had a kick-about at around 5.0 pm, then went to mass for 6.0. I said a few prayers that things would go well for me the next day! After that, it was down to Bellinter House for a bite to eat and our last big chat. Sean had it well structured and very well organised. It was short and sweet.

The instructions were a bit clearer for me for this game than for the Kerry game the year before! As a back, my first job was to defend first. I was going to be marking John O'Driscoll, who had been a schoolboy basketball International and I knew that John Kerins, who sadly passed away since, would aim a lot of kick outs at O'Driscoll.

I went home the night before thinking about him. I was focused on him, and only him. Sean would have had us that way – he had every player focused on who they were marking.

O'Driscoll had a big leap and was a great fielder of the ball. I didn't mind if he caught it, because I'd put him under pressure when he came down. Nowadays of course it'd be different because he'd be able to take the mark. But luckily enough, he never caught a ball that day. I played from behind and was able to break a few balls down, and I had a hand in our goal when I put him under a bit of pressure with my tackling.

We were lucky in that we're so near to Dublin. We slept in our own beds the night before, which was a big help and saved us from taking ourselves to strange hotel rooms. In 1987 we were staying in Malahide the night after the game, so we drove up there ourselves. The morning of any game I played for Meath, I'd get up around eight o'clock or half an hour later, and wash my car. That was my habit.

It was a superstition really, but also it was something to do. I was an early riser and Sean always said, 'There's no point lying in bed looking up at the ceiling... playing the game in your head. If you feel like getting up... get up.'

So that was how I was. I'd get up and have my breakfast and wash the car, whether it needed washing or not. I'd spend an hour cleaning it inside and out. My mother always had breakfast made for me. Toast, scrambled eggs, beans and a cup of tea.

I drove up to Dublin and brought Terry Ferguson with me. We had a quick meeting in the hotel where there were sandwiches laid on, but I would never eat much after I had my breakfast. I'd have a pink snack and a glass of water, and Gerry Mc was the same. I never ate any of the sandwiches that were going. I'd have the snack, and maybe another bar of chocolate and a banana for energy, and that was it.

We got the bus into Croke Park from Malahide, and of course we had the Garda escort, which was something new. *This is great... this is going to happen every year...* I told myself. Little did I know that it wouldn't! The crowds were huge. It reminded me of watching the FA Cup final when I was a young fella, watching the bus going through the crowds with the police escort. That's exactly what it was like.

I found out that the longer my career went on, the more nervous I got for big games. Sean always told us that nerves were good. But if you're too nervous, it can get on top of you. A little trick my mother had was she'd give me a little drop of brandy. I'm probably going to get her in trouble here, but she gave it to me when I was playing minor, and she kept at it! It was just a little mouthful, because I used to have elephants in my stomach, not butterflies, and it used to calm me down a small bit.

So I blame my mother for liking a few pints now and again! She never told my father or anyone.

'This is just between us,' she always said to me.

IN THE DRESSING-ROOM before the game, we all sat in our usual spots. We were up in Croke Park that often at that time that everyone had their preferred seat. Lads did their own thing. I used to get a rub down, but some lads wouldn't. The nerves in the dressing-room would have been serious, but once you got out onto the field, that went.

Sean brought us in close for a final chat, and everyone was raring to go. He kept it fairly simple. 'This is your stage… go out… and do your best'. We came out of the dressing-room with smiles on our faces. But we still had to march behind the Artane Boys Band before the game started. That had us all on our own, thinking about the game. It was always a long walk.

Sometimes in that moment I might pick out someone in the crowd whom I knew, and I'd be thinking about them. I'd be up on my toes and probably white as a ghost, but when that was done and we broke away from the band, I was back in the zone again. I picked up my position at left half-back in front of the Cusak Stand, shook hands with John O'Driscoll and took a deep breath.

I was ready.

In spite of the good build-up, we started the game really badly. After 20 minutes, we were 0-7 to 0-2 down. Things weren't going for us at all. The big turning point came just before that. Jimmy Kerrigan picked up a ball in the centre-forward position and ran about 30 yards – nobody laid a hand on him.

Just as Jimmy was winding up for a shot at goal, Mick Lyons came out of nowhere with this fantastic block. We went up the other end and got a score out of it, and that really turned things around for us. Soon after that, the ball came to John O'Driscoll, and I hassled and harried him and forced him into giving it away.

The breaking ball fell to David Beggy, who played it to Colm. He passed it across to Bernard Flynn, who tried to palm it in but it was blocked. We got a bit of luck as the ball fell to Colm and he was able to knock the rebound in with his fist.

If Kerrigan's shot had gone into the back of the net or over the bar, maybe things would have been different. But that block by Mick really was a turning point. Not taking away from him at all, but I think Kerrigan overplayed it a fraction, and that gave Mick that extra split-second to make the block. Soon after that, we were right back in the game. From the moment Colm's goal went in, we never looked back. Cork only scored three points in the second-half, and we ran out comfortable winners.

With about six minutes to go, they moved Terry Ferguson out to my position, took me off, and put Pádraig Lyons in. When I got to the sideline, all the lads in the dugout were shaking hands and hugging each other because they knew we had done it. I had a chance to take it all in because I was watching the last few minutes from the bench. It was a great feeling – but even now, when I look at the record books and it shows me being taken off, I'm not happy to see that! I don't know why they didn't take off Terry Ferguson for Pádraig – he was a corner back – like for like!

After the game, the scenes were just unbelievable. The crowd coming onto the field celebrating and congratulating us. It was amazing. I got more thumps on the field after the game than I did during it. Everyone was hugging us and jumping on us. I was thrilled for myself of course, but also for the lads who had been playing for Meath when nobody was following them - Mick, Gerry, Colm, Joe. To win it for them was great, and obviously for all my family and friends and people in the club. It was something I often dreamed about. I did nothing else but play football growing up, and now we had won the All-Ireland.

It's over 30 years ago now and I can still remember coming off the field and crowds hanging out of me. My family somehow found me out on the pitch. My father, my brothers. I had a couple of uncles too – Art and Matt - who lived in Dublin all their lives, and they were really proud of me.

The dressing-room after the game probably took an hour to clear. It was a free-for-all back then. Now it would be unheard of for so many people to be in the room – family, fans… you name it. All the players were hugging each other and different people were coming in and out and congratulating us. The Bishop of Meath, Michael Smith was also there with us after nearly every game. He was a good friend to the team.

Back at the hotel that night I crashed. It seemed like days since I had got out of my bed that same morning and washed the car. I had a few drinks and a bit of craic, but the next day was nearly more enjoyable because we were on the move – going here, going there. We weren't back in Navan until around midnight. Before that, we went to Dunboyne for Sean, then Summerhill because Mick was captain. So, we did an awful spin, and it was dead late when we got back to Navan.

On the Tuesday evening, a few of us met up in a quiet pub and the barman put on the video of the game. We'd great craic, all alone. Just ourselves. This was before smart phones, so nobody was putting up photos or videos of us and telling all their friends where the Meath lads were drinking. We were able to enjoy watching the game by ourselves and reflect on what we had achieved.

CHAPTER 8

THE BIG MONEY SPINNERS

"At a salary which brings in about 41 pence per minute, Taoiseach Charles Haughey's wage packet is puny compared with those of the world's top earners. Queen Elizabeth, for instance, earns £23 per minute, while American TV star Bill Cosby rakes in £32 million per year – a cool £213 a minute. Terry Wogan isn't in the super league – he earns a mere £3 a minute for his three nights a week on the box. Mr. Haughey can take some solace from the survey, though – his British counterpart Margaret Thatcher takes home only 15 pence a minute."

UGLY SCENES MAR KELLS TIE

"A virtual lynch mob drew battle lines outside every available exit from the playing pitch at Colmcille Park, Kells, yesterday when groups of supporters attempted to attack Sligo referee Mickey Kearins following Meath's narrow victory over Armagh in the National Football League. Eventually, he was rescued when players from both teams escorted Kearins to the dressing-room. This followed two earlier controversial decisions by the referee, who sent long-serving Meath forward, Colm O'Rourke to the line halfway through the second-half, and followed this up by dismissing Armagh's Jim McKerr just three minutes from the end."

The Irish Independent

WE WERE BACK out in the league a few weeks after the All-Ireland final. That Meath team never took a break. I know I never missed a league match unless I was injured. Maybe Colm O'Rourke and some of the older lads might have done so as the years went on, but very few of us opted out of games.

It's more common nowadays, when the likes of Dublin can have four or five lads to come back, but that was never the case with us. Maybe we'd have one or two to come back, but you could nearly name the team every week aside from a couple of lads. I think that stood to us big-time going on. Everyone wanted to put their shoulder to the wheel, everyone wanted to keep going on, and nobody wanted a break. Because we knew we'd be long enough looking in at it.

One of the worst injuries I ever got came against Armagh in the league at the back end of 1987. We had gone into that league campaign determined to keep the good run going. So, while Sean was introducing some new faces here and there – the likes of Mickey McDonnell and Brendan Reilly – it was pretty much the same core of the team that had won the All-Ireland. Páirc Tailteann was still out of action, so we were playing our home games in Kells, which had no stands or terraces, just a bank all the way around.

Half-way through the second-half of that game, the ball was going out for a '45' and I stupidly tried to keep it in. I ended up doing the splits, and I ripped every muscle going, from my knees up to my belly-button.

I was black and blue, and ended up in hospital for 10 days. The nurses had to bring me to and from bed, I couldn't put one foot in front of the other. When I eventually came back, someone recommended these bicycle shorts to me – which were new at the time – and I started wearing them, and I wore them until I finished. So that's how they came about – over me trying to stop a ball going out for a '45'! I think I started a trend with the blue bicycle shorts because Colm Coyle and Terry Ferguson started wearing them, too, and a lot of the Dublin lads copped on after that. Maybe I was a trend-setter!

That injury kept me out for about four months. In hindsight, that was no harm because I had been going non-stop for a long number of years at that stage. I loved it, but maybe the injury gave me the break I needed. We went to the Canaries in January of 1988 for our team holiday, and Sean would take me down to the sea. He was a great believer in the healing powers of the salt water. So while the boys were running the sand dunes, I was down in the water.

Picking close to our strongest team in the league paid off for us, with four wins from our seven games – including one against Kerry in Tralee. We drew two and lost one, so that was enough to put us through to a quarter-final against Louth, which we won narrowly. I was back for that game after the injury. We scraped over Down in Croke Park in the semi-final and Dublin beat Monaghan on the same day, so the scene was set for another battle between us.

I DON'T REMEMBER much about that league final which ended in a draw. We came back from behind in the last 10 minutes and actually took the lead, but Joe McNally got a late equaliser and brought the game to a replay. There was a bit of drama then over when the replay would be played.

Hill 16 was being renovated at the time, so that wasn't in use, and a suggestion to play the football final replay as part of a double-header with the National Hurling League final between Offaly and Tipperary was shot down because the GAA didn't think that Croke Park would be able to handle the crowds. Another option was to play our game on a Saturday, but that was knocked on the head because it was felt people would be in work and be unable to attend – it's hard to imagine such a concern being raised now. In the end, the GAA decided to have the replay after the upcoming All Star tour to the U.S., which meant there would be over a month between the drawn game and the replay.

The trip to the U.S. saw us play two games as All-Ireland champions against the All Stars. The first game was in Boston, the second was in San Francisco. We lost both, but there was an incident after one of the games between Kieran Duff and Kevin Foley. I had a habit of avoiding trouble so I don't know what happened, but whatever happened carried over into the rematch in Croke Park a couple of weeks later.

When we came back home from the States, we only had a week to prepare for the league final replay, but we trained hard when we were away and played a few games, there wasn't too much messing. The replay was a fairly bad-tempered game. The game wasn't that long on when Kevin was sent-off for an off-the-ball incident with Duff. There was a bit of a row and a couple of Dublin lads ended up on the ground, and Kevin got the line.

I saw footage of that game again recently, and my young lad said to me, 'Dad... look at the Dublin lads on the ground!' I told him they were just down with cramp.

We played some great stuff in that game and ended up winning handy enough. Liam Hayes got a great goal, straight from Mickey McQuillan's kick-out. He ran through and put it in the top corner down at the Canal End. We kept the winning habit going.

DESPITE THE FACT that it was generally the same 18 or 19 lads getting a run, the spirit was great, and everyone wanted to be involved. I never got any sense of fellas getting fed up because they weren't getting a run. It was great for me to have someone marking me in training who was pushing themselves hard, because that meant I pushed myself hard.

If a fella got the better of me in training, I would be under pressure for my place. We were all in that bubble and we all rowed the same way, there was nobody giving out. I put my hand up and admit that I was blessed to get back in after walking away, but I worked hard because there were lads chomping at the bit to get in. That's why I never stopped playing league, because I wanted to hold my place, and I'd say most lads were the same – they wanted to keep playing on and playing on… and playing on. A lot of us believed that if we were out for one match, we mightn't get back in that quick.

With the league final replay being pushed back until after the All Star trip, we only had a couple of weeks before we were back into the Leinster championship in early June. After winning the All-Ireland in 1987, we played the entire league with a final and a replay, and squeezed a trip to America in along the way, and we were on the road again for the 1988 campaign. It might have seemed like it was non-stop, and it was, but we all loved it. Everyone knew this wouldn't last forever.

The three in-a-row in Leinster was on, and Louth were our first opponents in Drogheda. That was a tasty atmosphere because there was the neighbourly rivalry between the counties, plus the fact that we were All-Ireland champions, so we weren't expecting to get anything easy. We met at The Neptune Hotel in Bettystown that morning and got the bus in. It was a scorching hot day, the pitch was so small, and the crowd was on top of us.

It was packed. We won comfortably in the end, but the downside was that we got a couple of injuries in that game. Brendan Reilly had come in for Kevin Foley, who was suspended after the league final, and he got a bad shoulder injury. Bernard Flynn got a knock as well. It was a tough, physical game because neither side was going to lie down. I remember coming off the field at the end and Jim McDonnell from Louth said to me, 'Martin, we've a long way to go to catch up to ye… ye're just unbelievable. How do ye keep going?' To hear that from an opponent was a great compliment, and I just shook his hand and said to him to just keep going. What else could I say?

We beat Offaly comfortably in Croke Park in the semi-final, and we were back in the Leinster final and yet another meeting with Dublin. We had played them so often in league and championship in the recent past, and there was a little bit of nastiness starting to creep in. There had been a few little schmozzles in several of the games, and of course the events of the National league final were still fresh in everyone's minds.

It was another Meath-Dublin game which wasn't a classic, and we definitely got the rub of the green. Hill 16 was still being upgraded, so the atmosphere was a little bit dead for a game of that size. We suffered a blow before the game when Brian Stafford was ruled out. PJ Gillic was given the job of hitting the frees, and he did well with them. We got two early goals and really they got us over the line because we only scored five points that day.

Dave Synnott was sent off for hitting Bernard Flynn, and those lads were best friends – they both worked with Tennent's. Synnott went off with a bloody nose for some reason. Everyone thought Bernard was a nice fella, but he had a few tricks of his own!

It looked like we were home and dry with time almost up, but Dublin got a penalty right at the end after Vinny Murphy was fouled. Mick Kennedy was Dublin's designated penalty taker at the time – a corner-back like Pádraig Lyons, you wouldn't see that much these days – but he was carrying a knock. Dublin nominated Charlie Redmond to take it and, thankfully, Charlie put it over the bar.

We were very lucky to come away from that one with the win. In a few of those Dublin games around that time, we got the luck. There was only a point or the hop of a ball between us most days. I was marking Declan Sheehan, who I'd come up against at minor level. Those games always came down to who made the fewest mistakes because there was so little between us. So things like that missed penalty went our way. But we felt that we had our share of bad luck over the years – missing our penalty in 1984 for example - and now we were starting to get it. The pendulum was starting to swing our way a bit.

THE DUBLIN GAMES were hammer and tongs from the first whistle. The difference in the pace of a game against Dublin versus, say, a game against Louth or Offaly back then was huge. You couldn't switch off for a second. They were better footballers, they were more physical... Dublin were the team to beat. We probably stopped them from winning a lot of things in that era.

We judged ourselves by how we did against Dublin and we always said that if we can get over them, we've a great chance of doing things. Sean drilled that into us. Once we got them on the floor, we wanted to keep our foot on their throat. We had massive respect for them and they would say the same about us, but we knew that they hated us, and we hated them! Mick Lyons would nearly take the door off the hinges going out – more so against Dublin than anyone else. It was like two rams banging heads against one another, and whoever was left standing at the end was the winner.

While there were a lot of incidents and melees in those games, I was able to keep my cool and stay out of trouble. I don't know why, but all the incidents at that time seemed to happen on the other side of the field from me. I was never on the end of a bad challenge or got set upon, so it was just one of those things. But we had a great balance in that team, and a few of us had to play a bit of football! Lyons, Harnan and Foley were the three lads who could do both – mix it and play football.

All I wanted to do was get the ball. Bob O'Malley, Terry Ferguson and myself were the three who'd play ball. I remember picking up loads of breaks, and Harnan was probably after sprawling two or three lads going for it, and the ball would break to me and I looked like a great lad. But Harnan was after killing a few lads just before!

It was the same in the forwards, we had three really brilliant footballers, and three lads who could do both. PJ could hit, O'Rourke could hit and Cassells could hit – and I don't mean that in the sense of being dirty – but they had the physical presence that any team needs. Then you had Flynn, Stafford and Beggy who could play ball.

I just played ball. Even with my club, I just wanted to play ball. I was never sent off, I'd say my name was only taken once or twice. Actually, I tell a lie, I was sent off once, but I was on the line at that stage! My son was playing an under-12 match in Dunsany, and I said something to the referee, and he sent me off. He gave me five minutes to get off too in fairness to him, because I wasn't going anywhere at first. But as a player I was never sent off.

If you look back at those games, if something happened it was usually in the area of the No. 6 or the No.5 or the No.3! Liam Harnan would often get the ball and the man. I remember an incident one year when he went for the man when he could have got the ball, and he got neither! He ended up taking out one of his own men, and I saw him doing that a few times. Sometimes I'd be shouting at him, 'Why didn't you go for the ball... you'd have got it!'

But Liam was man first, and then ball, whereas I was ball, then man! If Liam got both then it was a bonus. But Liam was great to play with – we needed him badly and when he wasn't there, it was more-or-less impossible to fill that gap to the same degree.

ONCE DUBLIN WERE out of the way, Mayo stood between us and another All-Ireland final. We were very comfortable in that game for most of it, until Mayo got two quick goals in the second-half and almost caught us.

We had to change strip for that as there was a colour clash, and we were wearing the yellow shirts and these really slick, shiny shorts. We were cruising, well and truly cruising. Then all of a sudden Mayo got their second goal and we had a bit of a nervous finish, but we got over the line. I'd say there was maybe a little bit of overconfidence creeping in for that game.

We were after winning three Leinsters in-a-row, and maybe we started to think we were unbeatable, which is the worst thing that can ever happen. In that Mayo game, we switched off big-time. The second goal brought it back to a three-point game, which woke us up. We tacked on a couple of points and won by five in the end.

That little rocky spell against Mayo gave us a bit of a kick up the backside, because we were back in an All-Ireland final and we were going to be playing Cork again. If we performed like we did against Mayo, it wasn't going to be nearly good enough. If we had run out fairly comfortable winners against Cork in 1987, we would soon find out that they were an entirely different animal 12 months later.

CHAPTER 9

MONDAY, SEPTEMBER 19, 1988

NOT-SO-GENTLE BEN LAYS DOWN GAUNTLET

"Get your money on Ben Johnson for his duel in the midday sun with Carl Lewis in the Olympic 100 metres final on Saturday. The Jamaican-born Canadian, with the muscles of a weightlifter, certainly has no doubts about the outcome of his clash with the American. 'When I'm at my best, no one can match me. No one will be with me at 60 metres,' he declared."

LARCENY ON THE GRANDEST POSSIBLE SCALE

Meath 0-12 Cork 1-9

"The old ground ought to have been sealed off as darkness enveloped its grimy precincts. Larceny had just been delivered on the grandest scale, or was it suicide? Either way, Cork pilgrims were stumbling about like grim-faced survivors of some calamitous deed. Mental smoke still billowed from their wreckage. Meath's throne could scarcely have taken a fiercer pounding had Hurricane Gilbert swept towards their goal. Yet, here it was intact and still imposing. So much for possession being nine tenths!"

The Irish Independent

WE PREPARED THE very same way as we did for the first All-Ireland. We got the press night out of the way, the clothes, and every possible distraction. We were creatures of habit, so we kept it exactly the same as the 1987 preparations. We knew it was going to be tough and we couldn't afford to take our foot off the pedal.

Especially with Cork being the team we'd beaten in the final the year before. If they were worth their salt at all, they were really going to be up for it big-time. Cork hadn't really performed in the '87 final, apart from the opening 25 minutes or so, and had a big point to prove. We were under no illusions and knew it would be even tougher in '88.

Billy Morgan had freshened up the Cork side and there were a few new

.ces in the team. In the forwards they had Paul McGrath and Mick McCarthy, who sadly passed away since. I was on McGrath and Bob O'Malley was on McCarthy. McGrath was only a young fella and I had watched a video of him playing, because I always looked extra close at lads I was marking. This lad was a flier.

I watched the Munster final and he was showing a clean pair of heels to everyone. So I knuckled down, I started doing some sprinting on my own at home in the back garden after training. Short sprints, five, 10, 20 yards. I'd put a ball down and sprint by it, then I'd go back and do it again, over and over. I did that right up until I was finished playing, and it definitely helped me. Paul McGrath put the fear of God into me with the pace he had, so I wanted to give myself every possible chance of sticking with him.

THE GAME STARTED really badly for us, once again, as Teddy McCarthy got a goal for Cork in the first few minutes. Dinny Allen skipped around a couple of challenges and played a lovely ball across the goal. McCarthy had slipped in behind our defence and stuck it between Mickey McQuillan's legs. The only thing you'd say about conceding that early was that we had plenty of time to get back into the game, and we were an experienced team so we didn't panic. We put the heads down, and got back into it with points.

But Cork really nailed us in that first game. Mick was down after an elbow to the head, Stafford got a split lip, and O'Rourke got an unmerciful shoulder from Barry Coffey under the Hogan Stand. To this day I think Colm would say that was the worst belt he ever got in a game – he was totally blindsided.

The Cork boys were in our faces and really up for it, probably even more so than we had expected. Maybe they feared us in '87, but they certainly didn't fear us this time. We realised early on that they were out to lay down a marker.

In the dressing-room at half-time, we all knew... *These boys are a different animal than they were 12 months ago.* Even if you look at the three lads who were hit, they were three of our main men. Whether that was talked about in the Cork camp, I don't know, but they were hitting us with everything they had, and we didn't get a minute on the ball. We didn't play well at all. Cork threw us off our stride with their approach, I think that's fair to say. Luckily, we got out of it with a draw in the end.

Larry Tompkins hit an almighty free into the Canal End to put Cork ahead with time almost up, and it looked like we were beaten. McQuillan got the kick-out away and it broke off a Cork man and went out for a sideline in front of the Cork bench over on the Cusack Stand side.

I took it, and it broke off a mass of bodies around 21 yards out from the Cork goal. David Beggy got onto it, hit the deck in the crowd, and Tommy Sugrue gave the free in.

To this day it's controversial. It probably didn't help that Tommy was from Kerry. But I know Tommy was always adamant that there was a foul. To be balanced about it, the free that Cork got to put them ahead, I thought that was really soft. But that doesn't get as much attention as that free right at the end.

Beggy would say it was a foul, but if you look at it, I'd have to be honest and say it appears to be a bit soft. If it had been given against us, we'd have been raging, too, just like Cork. Stafford stuck it over. Just! So we got the draw out of it. In the dressing-room, there was a lot of relief and a lot of sore bodies.

We definitely had luck on our side.

In the days after that game, the conversation was really about one thing. With what had happened with Mick and the lads, we knew Cork had bullied us, they shoved us around. We promised ourselves that the same would not happen in the replay. Maybe we went over the top a little bit in the replay, but we certainly weren't bullied because there was no way that was going to be allowed to happen twice in-a-row.

There wasn't really that much said in the run up to the replay. It just took the Monday morning and Tuesday night after the drawn game for us to get our thoughts together. We had a really good night on the Sunday. You'd think we had won it with the night we had! The next morning, Sean addressed us. The tone of that meeting was very much that we were bullied and Cork didn't fear us, and that they had their homework done.

Sean was very good at getting through to us, a few little words from him and everyone knew exactly what had to be done. It was all very calm, there was no effing and blinding or lads standing up losing their cool. We just took everything in, and we knew ourselves what we needed to do.

The Tuesday night after training was much the same again in the meeting we had, refresh the minds. We didn't know when the replay was going to be – in the end it took three weeks. Then there was talk that Liam Hayes would be going away to cover the Olympic Games in Seoul for the *Sunday Press*. We were all worried he was going to miss the replay, we thought he might have no choice but to go given it was his job. Thankfully, he reached a compromise with his bosses and he didn't head to Seoul. He was colossal for us, so he'd have been a huge miss.

IN THE WEEKS between the two games, we talked amongst ourselves. It wouldn't always have been coming from Sean. We looked at the video, and we picked out several things that happened and said it wouldn't happen again. The weekend before the match, we went up to Dundalk and stayed in the Ballymacscanlon Hotel. We trained in Cooley Kickhams' pitch on the Saturday, had a few drinks on the Saturday night, without going too mad, and we had a training game on the Sunday morning. We got a referee from Louth in to do it. After 15 minutes, Sean ran on and abandoned it.

We were killing each other.

Kevin Foley went off with a sore knee.

Hayes nailed McEntee... all hell broke loose.

So, Sean ran in, the ref blew it up, and we all headed for the dressing-room.

THE TONE WAS set, and I don't mean that we were hell-bent on going out to take the heads off lads the following Sunday, but we were ready.

Sean didn't say anything to us after. We just togged in and headed home... 'See yis on Tuesday night'. There were a few locals there watching the game, and they must have been thinking... *My God... these lads are lunatics.*

I'd say they couldn't believe what was going on, lads knocking lumps out of one another a week before an All-Ireland final. As usual for me, all the incidents seemed to happen away from where I was standing. It had to be stopped, because lads were so geared up.

Watching the video back brought everything home in very clear terms.

Maybe I didn't see a particular incident during the game, but when I watched the video back, I could see it all and that stuck in my head. But we just looked at it once. That was enough. Of course, we knew we had to up our game as well without being bullied. Not too many of us played well in the drawn game. We just didn't perform.

We were back training in Dalgan on the Tuesday night. Thankfully, there was no repeat of the blow-out that happened in Cooley. That wouldn't have been ideal for our own supporters to see, but I'm sure news had travelled back from Louth as to what happened. Thankfully this was a time before social media and smart phones! I can only imagine the furore if someone had footage of that game and it did the rounds.

We made three changes for the replay. Pádraig Lyons, Kevin Foley and Mattie McCabe were dropped. It was really tough on those lads. Sean named the team in front of us all, as usual, but he would have gone to the three lads first to let them know. Coyler, Terry Ferguson and Joe Cassells came back in.

Joe had been injured earlier in the year but he was just coming right. Coyler wasn't that long back from Chicago. He played in the Leinster final because Stafford was injured, and came on against Mayo. Sean was ruthless when he needed to be. I really felt for the three lads who lost out, because I would certainly have hated to be dropped. I wasn't too worried because I thought I had done okay in the drawn game. But that game in Louth the week before, I don't know what Sean saw but he obviously saw something in that 15 minutes, or maybe he had his mind made up already.

The only bit of controversy was Coyler getting back in because he had been away – a bit like me when I left and came back. But he was a class footballer. Terry maybe just had a touch more pace than Pádraig, and Joe had the bit of experience. That's just my take on it, I couldn't tell you exactly what Sean was thinking. But, really, it didn't bother me who was playing. We were going out to win the game and that was it.

In the dressing-room before the game, lads were really up for it, more so than usual – Gerry especially. We were walking behind the band and Gerry would have been two behind me, and I remember turning to pass the water bottle back and he was actually marching – the knees were up and the arms were going. He was all out for it.

While I wasn't involved directly in the controversy in either game, one little coincidence was that the major incidents in each game came from sideline balls that I took from in front of the Cork dugout. In the drawn game, I hit the ball in that resulted in us getting the late free. In the replay, the game was only on six minutes when a sideline ball I hit broke off PJ Gillic to Niall Cahalane. Gerry gave Niall Cahalane a bit of a wallop, and Cahalane went down like a sack of spuds!

He'd always admit that Gerry didn't hit him that hard, but he lay down. Then everyone was in! For once it was on my side, but it was 50 yards further up the field. I ran down, but by the time I got there it was nearly all over. It was mostly handbags, but the belt Gerry threw was seen, and that's what he got done for. I saw the referee talking to Gerry, so I went across to plead with the ref.

I was telling him that he couldn't just send off one when there were four or five involved. Gerry was pleading, but it didn't do too much good! Up went the hand from the referee… GONE!

It was just unfortunate for Gerry, he was wound up and he got caught.

I just shrugged my shoulders and walked away. You don't really have much time to think about it, you just have to put the shoulder to the wheel. I still thought we could do it, we had to think positive. There was no point in thinking… *Jesus, what are we gonna do now?* I was positive enough that we could still do it once everyone raised their game, and everyone did. Cork people won't mind me saying that Colm O'Rourke got away with murder that day. He would admit that himself. He brought Paul McGrath down at one stage – rugby tackled him under the Hogan Stand – and the referee gave a free to Meath!

At another time in the game, I think the referee was pulling the notebook to book him – Colm ran off, and the notebook went back into the pocket. O'Rourke refereed that game. He played brilliantly, and he refereed it. He was in the referee's ear for a lot of the game. Nowadays he'd probably have been sent off!

Near the end of the game I took another sideline in front of the Hogan Stand, in front of the presentation area. Colm got it, threw a couple of lads out of the way and stuck it over with his right foot, and he gave the little fist pump.

When I saw that going over, I thought… *Well if O'Rourke can knock one over with his right foot, we're going to win this game.*

That put us four points up with seven or eight minutes left. Then the pressure really came on from Cork. With 10 minutes to go, I was out on my feet. Absolutely exhausted. For the last five minutes or so, Cork started pumping balls in, and we were really hanging on. Balls broke to me, and I just kicked them as far as I could, because Mick Lyons was roaring.

'GET IT OUT OF THERE!

'GET IT OUT OF THERE!'

I wasn't playing around with it. Now, it might have gone 60 yards, but it went straight into a Cork fella's hands, and then it came straight back in. So I'd get another one, and I'd kick that back out… it was like kicking a ball against a wall. I couldn't run with it because I was so knackered, all I could do was kick it. If I had run with it and got caught with it, we'd have been in trouble. So at least kicking it took the pressure off for a few seconds and we could regroup, because we had a lot of bodies back.

While I was booting it clear, Coyler got one ball, tapped it on his toe, went by a fella and won a free. *Why couldn't I have done that?* I thought to myself. Instead I took my orders from Mick!

Looking back, I really should have tried to find a man and keep the ball, because Cork had two lads waiting around the middle. They got a few points, but once they didn't score a goal, I think we felt we were going win it.

They got it back to a point, then that was it.

It was over. We rode our luck a bit, but we got there. I've never felt as tired at the end of a game. A lot of that was down to the extra man and the extra running we had to do.

Winning any All-Ireland is special. Winning the first one was unbelievable, but to win a second was just fantastic. But it's funny, as tight as those games were, I never felt we were going to lose it in either match. Having said that, I thought this was going to be the way for the rest of my career – winning All-Irelands.

It wasn't quite like that! So maybe I was being a little optimistic in thinking we wouldn't lose. That was how it turned out, of course, but Cork could easily have won either of those games – especially the drawn game.

AFTER THAT REPLAY in 1988, the main feeling was one of relief. Well, relief and exhaustion. To win it with 14 men and to win it for Gerry McEntee was huge.

Everyone was delighted for Gerry, because we all felt bad for him. At the time we were probably thinking… *What the fuck were you doing?* But these spur of the moment things happen. We got across the line without him. And to win two in-a-row, and to win it the way we did, made it even better than the first one.

Along with winning the All-Ireland, I won the Man of the Match award. For me to get picked was a great thing from a personal perspective, but I said in the dressing-room after that it should have been 'Team of the Match'. Everyone should have got an award. The way everyone put their shoulder to the wheel, put their bodies on the line… it was just incredible.

The only thing which disappointed me slightly was the Man of the Match award was given to me in the dressing-room after the game.. It should have been done at the hotel that night. I think it was the late Enda Colleran who selected me. So it was presented to me in the dressing-room, I said a few words, and that was it. We went back to the hotel in Malahide that night, and everyone was waiting for the Man of the Match to be announced, and nobody knew who got it. I think someone had to announce that I received it, hours earlier! My mother and father, and Samantha and a few of the family were back in the hotel, but none of them knew.

The fall-out from that game wasn't great. Papers ran stories which accused us of bringing shame on the GAA. On top of that, at the reception for both teams in the Royal Hospital, Kilmainham the day after the replay, the then President of the GAA, John Dowling said that he was not 'totally satisfied with certain happenings on the field'.

'This is not the occasion to deal with them,' Dowling added. 'I shall deal with them at an appropriate place and time.' A lot of lads took that to heart.

At the medal presentation later that winter in Warrenstown College Dowling was there to present the All-Ireland medals, and Harnan and Gerry wouldn't go up to collect theirs. We thought that either everyone should go up, or no-one should go up. Maybe you could say that the rest of us chickened out of it, but the two lads stuck to their guns. I went up to get mine, because the way I looked at it, I might never get another one.

It was the individual decision of each man and that was it. But the first game was every bit as bad as the replay, and there was nothing said after that game. So I think that's why some of the lads were a little bit annoyed. In the replay, aside from that one incident for the sending off, there wasn't much in it. But in the first game, we had two or three lads floored and we didn't give out, and neither did the President of the GAA.

I DON'T KNOW whether it was because of the media or what, but there was a genuine dislike between the Meath and Cork lads at that time. At the function in Kilmainham the day after the game, there was very little said by any of the Meath lads to the Cork boys, and vice-versa.

It's only as the years passed that we realised how stupid we all were. In January of 1989 we went to the Canaries for a holiday. Everything was paid for and we were damn glad to get it. What we didn't know was that Cork were going the same two weeks as ourselves. Not alone that, but they were staying in the same hotel as us! So that was a little bit… awkward.

We were one side of the pool, they were the other.

We never spoke. When you think back on it, it was shocking, absolutely shocking. We were thick, and they were twice as thick – or take your pick! You'd see three or four Cork lads going up to the bar, and you'd wait your turn. They'd come back down, then we'd go up.

I wouldn't have minded saying hello but it just turned into a big stand-off, and nobody wanted to break it. But it was just so childish, so stupid.

But that's football, and that's the way it was.

Sadly, it took a tragedy to get us all talking again. That was when John Kerins passed away and the whole lot of us went down to his funeral. It took something like that for everyone to realise that there was a lot more to life than football.

CHAPTER **10**

MONDAY, OCTOBER 24, 1988

HOTELS CALL TIME ON 'DEBS' DRINKING SESSIONS

"New guidelines issued by the Irish Hotels Federation will lead to stricter control on the supply of alcoholic drinks at debs dances and other teenage social functions, according to the federation's president, Mr. Peter Malone. The federation, which was one of the major campaigners for the introduction of longer licensing hours, has asked its members to be particularly vigilant about the serving of alcohol to teenagers at debs functions. The battle against teenage alcohol abuse was being won slowly, Mr. Malone said, through various means. As well as stricter controls on alcohol, an increasing number of parents were now attending debs dances."

MEATH SOUNDLY BEATEN BY MONAGHAN
Monaghan 3-12 Meath 2-9

"If it is Meath's intention to retain, or try to retain, the Royal Liver National Football League title, more than 7,000 spectators saw no evidence of it at Páirc Tailteann, Navan, yesterday. In this first-round game of the new competition, the dual champions were soundly beaten by Monaghan, who led by 12 points twice in the second-half and finished the hour with a comfortable margin of six. Meath fielded only nine of their All-Ireland winning team… and with the exception of Liam Smith… none of the replacements seriously challenged for places in future fixtures."

The Irish Times

WITH THE REPLAY of the 1988 All-Ireland final happening in October, it meant that we really didn't get much of a break before the league started up again. To score 2-9 against Monaghan in that opening game wasn't too bad given all the celebrating we had done.

A few of the older lads had taken a bit of a break – Mick, Colm and a few others. So we were throwing lads in who, though they had been on the panel for a while, hadn't really played a whole lot. In the championship we were working with 18 or 19 lads, so outside of that, a lot of the other lads on the panel weren't getting too many opportunities. It made it much harder for them to make an impression when they did get a chance, because they just weren't used to it. So, while we were doing well, we were using a fairly small group of players. If there were any big injuries, we would struggle to cope with that. That was something we would find out to our cost in 1989.

In my opinion, Sean was right to focus on the 15 and then the three or four lads who came in and out. It was hard for lads to get in, and if they did get in and get a chance, they'd have to play really well. If they did, Sean would always come back to them.

Whether that was right or not, I don't know. But when you look back on it, we won a lot, so he was probably right. A lot of people say we should have won more, and maybe we should have. But we were lucky on some occasions and unlucky on others. Me, I think that team probably deserved to win another one or two All-Irelands at least.

THAT LEAGUE CAMPAIGN of 1988-89, the likes of Gerry Martyn, Packie Henry, Liam Smith and Alan Browne played quite a bit. They probably felt though, that no matter how well they played, they were always going to be pushed aside when the old lads came back. I have to say, all those lads really helped us.

In terms of training, I took a break after the last game of the league before Christmas. If we had won the All-Ireland, we'd go on holidays in early January, then we'd be back for the restart of the league. So that was really the only break I'd have taken. Although, even on holidays, Sean would always do a bit of training with us.

Sean would never let you know early in the night. Instead, there'd be a note left under your door in the hotel, and we'd arrive in at whatever time – two, three or four o'clock in the morning. So you'd see this little note on the ground and you'd pick it up and read it – and some lads would barely be in a state to read it! And it would say… "See you in the lobby at half seven for training".

FUCK! TRAINING AT HALF SEVEN!
Why didn't he tell us earlier?

But that's how Sean was, he'd surprise us. There'd be a lot of sick heads, but lads got on and you just did it, you got on with it. We used to run on the sand dunes – Sean loved sand dunes – and even at that time of the morning we'd be sweating. We might go around the dunes a few times and maybe a couple of lads would hide and then re-join when we came back around, but Sean would never say anything at the time.

When we got back to the hotel though, he would name the few lads who ducked out – he never missed anything – but that was all part of the craic. Definitely though, not too many lads were too fond of the half seven starts… there weren't a lot of prayers said for Sean at that time!

THE LEAGUE DIDN'T go too well for us, and we were relegated.

I don't think anyone was too concerned about that, but then before the Leinster championship, Mick broke his leg. He was a huge loss. A lot of lads were nearly afraid to go in around the goal because Mick had such a presence – he owned the square.

I remember coming home after hearing about the injury and thinking… *Jesus, we won't have Mick!!!!*

But Sean always drilled it into us to just get on with it. No matter what, you get on with it. Mick was only one man, but he was a huge, huge loss. We played a challenge match against Kildare in Summerhill a few weeks before the championship, and we didn't score the whole game. I don't think I've ever played another game for club or county when that happened. Meath fans were probably getting worried, but Sean was after running the bollocks off of us the previous… I think it could have been 10 or 12 nights in-a-row. We really trained hard, and in that game the legs were like jelly. But not to score was unreal.

Going into the championship, we had to rejig things a bit. Joe Cassells played full-back the first day against Louth. Joe wouldn't have played there too much in his career, but it was a case of needs must. He played corner-back in 1986, but that was to pick up Tommy Carr in the Leinster final, because Tommy would roam out the field. To put him in full-back didn't suit him, but Sean had to try something. A manager has to look at his options.

In the Leinster semi-final against Offaly, Bob O'Malley played full-back, so we were taking probably the best corner-back in the country at the time and moving him. You probably lose more than you gain in that instance. For the Leinster final, against Dublin again, Harnan was given the job of trying to fill Mick's position, but he was never really that comfortable at full-back. It's a really tough place to play.

If it was any other position on the field, you might get away with it – like putting a centre-back into midfield or a wing-back to wing-forward. Full-back is different. Then when you add Mick's presence to that – it was a big hole to fill and we ended up robbing Peter to pay Paul.

The whole defence was upset because of one position. We were moving Harnan from centre-back or O'Malley from the corner to try to paper over the cracks, and that left us weaker across the whole defence. Mick just had that fear factor. He wasn't dirty, I think he was only sent off once in his career. Or maybe he only got caught once! He was a huge name. Even today, Mick's name is known the length and breadth of Ireland.

It's a great name, too, Lyons' den and all that, and Mick probably knew that and it helped him build that reputation. Mick was a quiet, shy fella. He didn't like the limelight or doing interviews. Inside the dressing-room though, he was very vocal, very straight.

That 1989 Leinster final was played on a really hot day. I was wing back. Kieran Duff got that famous goal early on. He got away with about 25 steps, and stuck a brilliant shot into the top corner. It was a typically tight game. Mattie McCabe got a goal with about 10 minutes left which put us a point up, and I looked over to the sideline and I saw Mick warming up, and I thought… *Now is the time to bring him on.*

I think it would given us a huge lift and maybe knock some of the stuffing out of Dublin. Only Jack Finn and Sean would have known if Mick was one hundred percent right to come on. Maybe it was just a bit of psychology to get him out warming up and let Dublin see him. Whatever, he didn't come on.

Everything they hit after that went over. Joe McNally kicked one from under the Cusack Stand over his left shoulder. Now, Joe was a fine footballer, but he probably wouldn't have done it if they were a point down! So they were on a bit of a roll at that stage and Vinnie Murphey scored a goal that came off my elbow. That was the turning point and they ended up winning by five in the end.

I remember thinking the ref was a bit hard on us. It was Sean Kelly from Carlow, who I'd never heard of before or since. It would have been a huge one to win, because we always felt that if we got over Dublin, we'd go on to win another All-Ireland. There was a fire behind the Nally Stand in that game, too, and smoke was blowing across the pitch. It was only a pity the fire didn't stop the game, because if it had been two weeks later, I'd say Mick might have been right.

He had worked so hard to get back after breaking the leg. I remember him coming into training, and Gerry McEntee had gotten him some kind of hinge on the plaster so that he was able to cycle the bike. He kept his training up that way, and was really keen to get back. I'd say another two weeks, he would have been okay.

WE'D BEEN ON the go pretty much for four years at that stage, without much of a break. People might think that maybe there was a bit of relief that the year was over earlier than normal. I can assure you, there was never any relief when you'd been beaten by Dublin. We were going all out for three All-Irelands in-a-row, not to mention four Leinsters.

Unfortunately, it didn't work out.

In spite of that disappointment with Meath, 1989 wasn't a total dead loss for me, as I won the Intermediate championship with St Michael's. We were after winning the Junior back in 1982, so it took us a few years to get to grips with the Intermediate championship. The club was probably delighted that Meath were knocked out early! Maybe it was no coincidence that we won when I was back training regularly with the club, and maybe I was being selfish and greedy only thinking of the county, but you tried your best to keep everyone happy. We played Dunderry in the final in Navan. They were after losing the previous two finals, so we knew they'd be hard beaten. Tommy Dowd was in America and they brought him home for that match.

There was a great character in our club called Mick 'The Hay' Smith. Lord rest him, he was a farmer and he used to cut hay and that's where the name came from. We played with a gale-force wind in the first-half, but went in two points down at half-time, so it wasn't looking too good for us. Mick was a bit of a gambler, and he pulled £200 out of his pocket at half-time and had a bet with someone from Dunderry – don't ask me who – that St Michael's would win the game. And he was right! We beat them by two points in the end.

It was a low-scoring game. Seán Kelly, who went on to play for Meath, had a chance at the end to score a goal, but he pulled it wide. There were four of us O'Connells playing in that final – myself, Robert, Michael and Pat. Robert scored four or five points that day – he couldn't miss – and I scored two. My brother Michael was full-forward. He was a great target man, and then Pat marked Tommy Dowd.

Even now, Tommy is asked who was the dirtiest player he ever played on, and he always mentions my brother, Pat – and remember, this is a man who has marked Keith Barr! Pat would never come out in front to win the ball or get a hand in. He'd always let his man win it and then thump the ribs off him – but he'd get away with it. Tommy would tell you that. Everywhere he went that day, he got the ribs thumped off him. That was the way Pat played. You wouldn't get away with it now, but it was a lot different back then.

Robert was an outstanding footballer. He won an All-Ireland medal with the Meath Juniors in 1988 playing in goals, but was very unlucky not to get onto the Meath senior team. He played in the O'Byrne Cup final in '83, but then he got a very bad injury. We were after opening the pitch down in Carlanstown, and played a challenge match before it was officially opened. Robert fell on a stone and split his kneecap wide open, and it took him a long, long time to get over it. He probably would have been on that Meath team in 1987 and '88 had it not been for that injury. That's how good I reckon he was. He was a brilliant free-taker, and he could sell a dummy. He was another Colm O'Rourke and another Brian Stafford. I have to say he was as good if not better than that, and if you'd asked a lot of lads around the county, they'd say Robert was better than me.

We were different footballers, but Robert was the key man for the club and he was very unlucky he didn't make the county.

CHAPTER **11**

COST OF FLYING HIGH

"The boom in commercial aviation has also swelled the ranks of Irish high-fliers. Top executives now think nothing of chartering a private plane to nip across the channel to high-level financial meetings. Taking a chopper jaunt to the race track or hopping round the top hotels by helicopter for the weekend is also the order of the day. Among those using private craft are Dr. Michael Smurfit, Dr. Tony O'Reilly, Larry Goodman, Chris De Burgh and Ossie Kilkenny."

MEATH BACK IN BUSINESS
Meath 2-7 Down 0-11

"The sabbatical has ended. Meath are back in business and carrying it out without the pomp and ceremony of yore, but with an endeavour which makes them the leading side in the country. All the other counties will have watched the new Royal Liver League champions with trepidation at Croke Park yesterday. Brave Down provided them with the most severe test. Sean Boylan's merry band of men passed with honours."

The Irish Independent

I MET SAMANTHA in 1989.

On our first date, I brought her to Roscommon, to a league game in Kiltoom. Who said romance is dead? We were beaten by 16 points. There wasn't much chat going home, I can tell you that. Then a couple of weeks later, Antrim hammered us by 10 points. So Samantha definitely wasn't a lucky charm at the start!

Somehow, we made it through the knockout stages of the league and beat Cork in the semi-final. There was a little bit of niggle to that game, and Niall Cahalane was sent-off for pushing Colm into the hoardings in front of the Cusack Stand. The GAA trialled new rules during that league, some of which survived and are now part of the game. Matches were divided up into four quarters of 15 minutes, frees could be taken from the hands, while sidelines and kick-outs *had* to be taken from the hands.

We met Down in the league final. We didn't really know too much about them before that game, and we just went into it with our own game in mind. We started fairly slowly but David Beggy got a great goal into the Hill which got us going, and Stafford scored a penalty near the end to get us over the line.

I was marking Ambrose Rodgers that day, who sadly passed away in 1999. He was only 39. I don't remember a huge amount about that league final, but I remember marking Ambrose in a game up in Newry a few years before. I was coming out for a ball, and he gave me a bit of an elbow to the back of the head. I went face first into a huge puddle of water, the ref played on, and by the time I got up the ball was in the net! So he got one belt at me at least! It was very sad for his family to see him die at such a young age.

One other unusual thing which happened in that league final was Tommy Sugrue – our old friend from 1988 – took off his boots at some point and refereed a lot of it in his socks. Tommy must have packed the long studs instead of the 'moulded' that morning! Mick Lyons was back to full fitness and back on the edge of the square, so winning that final was a great boost to get going into the championship. Of course, we would cross paths with Down again in the not-too-distant future.

WE MADE IT through to the Leinster final without much difficulty where, for the fifth year in-a-row, we met Dublin. We had been without Mick in 1989, and in 1990 we were missing Liam Harnan due to a back problem. So, for the second year running, we were without one of the lynch-pins in our defence. I was named at centre-back, but Foley moved in there at the start of that game. I might have been there for the National anthem – Sean always had this thing that you stood in your 'named' position for the national anthem – but as soon as the game started, you'd change. It was the same with Dublin. We'd see the Dublin team in the paper or in the programme, and we'd know that they weren't going to line out that way, and nine times out of 10, they didn't.

Sean would have his team named, and whoever came over, that's who I picked up. The Dublin forwards would always change. So if I looked at the programme and Charlie Redmond was named at centre-forward, I would know that he wasn't going to play there. Sean always said, 'Whoever comes over… you pick them up'. Then he'd make changes if needed during the game.

While the management might make switches during a game, the key thing for us was that Mick *always* had to be left on the edge of the square. Teams would try to pull him out by moving the full-forward out the field or whatever, but one thing we would never do was move Mick out. He stayed there and someone else would pick up his man if that's what was needed. Things are a bit different now, but back then the edge of the square was a place that you wanted your best man, and our best man was Mick Lyons.

We got the perfect start in that game. Straight from the throw-in, Colm went up for a dropping ball with John O'Leary. It was just a big, high ball into the square from Colm Brady, and O'Rourke went up for it with one eye on the ball and one eye on O'Leary. The ball ended up in the net and the goal was given. Whether it would be given now, I don't know. I have my doubts.

O'Leary kind of had it on his chest and the ball bounced off him, hit O'Rourke, went into the net, and the goal was given. It was a great start for us, and we went in five points up at half-time, which didn't happen too often against Dublin. I kicked a point in the first-half, which didn't happen too often either! Bernard Flynn was always slagging me for kicking high balls into him. Well, he got the ball under the Cusack Stand and he never even looked! He just kicked a high ball across the field up in the air, and it just happened to fall into my hands, and I kicked it over the bar from around the '45'. We were in good shape at half-time. In the end though, we were hanging on a bit.

Leo Close and Barney Rock came on and both played really well, and helped get Dublin back into it. They whittled it back to a point and, all of a sudden, we were in a bit of a battle. Thankfully, we rallied well in the last five minutes. I set up Stafford for a point, and Beggy kicked one and we held on. Keith Barr kicked a massive point from a sideline at one stage – you talk about Maurice Fitzgerald, but Keith hit this ball, and I didn't think he'd even make the 21 yard line with it.

The next thing is, he winds up and it sails over the black spot. They got some great scores to bring them right back into it, but we finished well. Colm O'Rourke was captain that year, even though Skryne weren't county champions. Sean pushed for that change to be made – that it didn't have to be someone from the county champions that captained the team. It was the right thing to do, too, because Colm deserved his time as captain. It was great to see him lifting the Leinster trophy, and great to get our title back after slipping up in '89.

Donegal were the opposition in the semi-final. Ulster was so competitive at that time, as it still is, so whoever came out of it were going to be battle-hardened. Going into that game, we knew the threat they were going to be because they had some fantastic attackers. They had Martin and James McHugh, Joyce McMullan, Tony Boyle, Manus Boyle and Declan Bonner. That was a serious forward line by any standards. Martin McHugh was their play-maker. They were fit, they could score, and they'd hammered us in the league in '88. Martin McHugh scored nine points that day, so we were well aware of their threat.

It was a tough, tough match. We got a few goals at the right time to win it. Bernard Flynn got two – one of them hit the post and went in off the keeper. Brian Stafford got the other one when he just pulled on a loose ball, so we got the goals when we needed them. We came out battered and bruised that day, but we just about got across the line. It was a really wet day, and we were in our Leinster colours of green and white. Donegal were wearing the gold and black that Ulster teams wear.

THE LATE LIAM Creavin was the secretary of the county board at that time, but his wife, Ita was the real secretary, we used to say! Ita would hand out the tickets for the All-Irelands. Her head must have been fried. She was a lovely, kind, good-hearted woman but she had a whole county to keep under manners at times. She used to give out the togs and socks for the games aswell.

Liam came to training one of the nights before the Donegal game with the Leinster togs and socks – the green and white. I got this pair of socks off Liam and I don't know what size they were, but I went home with them anyway. Sean always told us to wash the bottom of the socks because they'd cut your feet otherwise. So before I washed them, I put them on, and they were like a pair of tights. They came right up to my thigh.

Jesus, I can't play in these.

I always tried the gear on the night before the game, to make sure I'd be comfortable. I said to myself that I'd ring Ita, because she must have given me the wrong size. I had to pluck up a bit of courage, because I knew I wasn't going to get too warm a reception.

I rang her up anyway, and she said, 'Yes, Martin?'

'Ita,' I began, 'I'm just wondering about the size of the socks we got last night – they're like a pair of tights.'

Ita wasn't happy with my complaint.

'What do you think this is, Martin… a sports shop?'

As soon as I heard that, I said, 'That's grand' and I dropped the phone. I wore the socks the next day. I washed them a few times, and I wore them with another pair underneath.

I DIDN'T HAVE much time to worry about the gear once we went onto the field, but we got on top in the half-back line, and James and Martin McHugh were both taken off. We kept them scoreless from play.

Martin was the big threat, but Foley kept him fairly quiet. We knew that the Donegal forwards would cause us trouble if we didn't get our act together, but fortunately we did. It was very physical, and we came out of it with a few knocks. We beat them by eight points in the end, but the scoreboard made it look a lot more comfortable than it actually was. We got the two goals in the second-half, very close together. Stafford got his and then a few minutes later, Hayes set Flynn up and that was that really it.

We were back in the All-Ireland final, and once again it's Cork who were waiting for us. I really think what cost us in that game was there was an element of… *We've beaten them before… we'll beat them again.*

Once you start thinking like that, it's hard to drag yourself out of that mind-set. It's easy saying it now, and Sean probably thought we were in the right frame of mind, but deep down, I thought we took them for granted for

My First Holy Communion, with a whole lot of wars to be won and lost on the football fields all ahead of me.

With Samantha, my mother and father, and all the O'Connell gang celebrating my selection on the GAA's Team of the Millennium (top). My father keeping manners on us in our younger days (centre) and me on my trusty little Honda during my schooldays.

Samantha and I on our wedding day (top) when we had little idea of the times ahead. We got to travel the world thanks to my football career.

Samantha and I have been lucky to enjoy watching our amazing kids (Brian, Barry and Jane) grow into adults of whom we are so proud.

*Playing with St Michael's, whether
I won or lost, was always the
greatest joy of my life. And we
won occasionally (bottom) as I
celebrate with Barry in my arms.*

I've been allowed to feel on top of the world in two different decades thanks to two separate Meath teams and our always loyal supporters. Here I am hoisted high in 1987 after we defeated Cork in the All-Ireland final, and again in 1996 (bottom) after we finally got by Mayo after an infamous replay.

The Meath team that defeated Cork in the 1987 All-Ireland final.

So much about my career was all about Dublin, our toughest and greatest of neighbours. I break the ball down in our epic four-game battle with them in 1991 (top) and chase down Vinny Murphy four years later (below). I also got to captain Meath when we played against them.

Playing full-back on the team that won the National league title in 1994 was a huge moment for me (top) and getting to play with so many magnificent young players on that new Meath team was a massive bonus for me, but it did mean I had to train even harder.

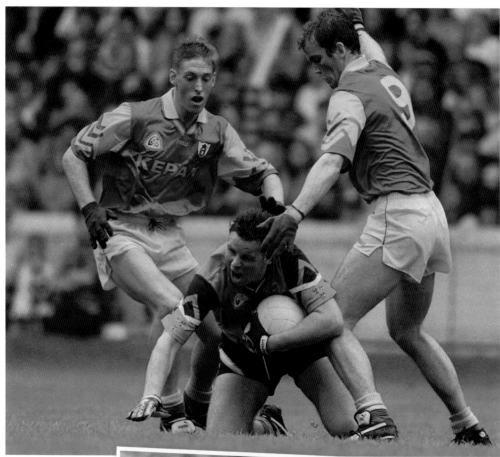

There was a huge hunger about the second Meath team that Sean Boylan built and I knew we would not have to wait around long to win things. Trevor Giles and John McDermott (top) dominate against Dublin in the 1996 Leinster final and (below) John Mc is still laying down the law against Tyrone in the All-Ireland semi-final the same summer.

The Meath team that defeated Mayo and was crowned All-Ireland champs in 1996.

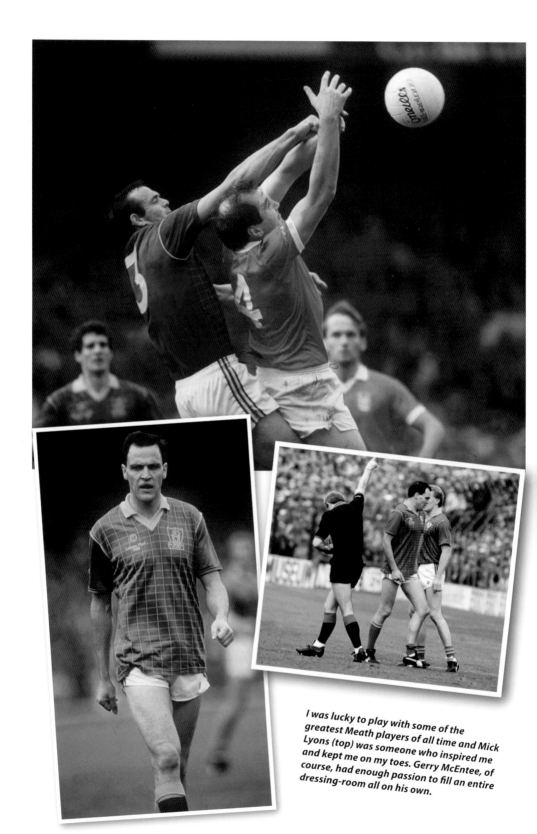

I was lucky to play with some of the greatest Meath players of all time and Mick Lyons (top) was someone who inspired me and kept me on my toes. Gerry McEntee, of course, had enough passion to fill an entire dressing-room all on his own.

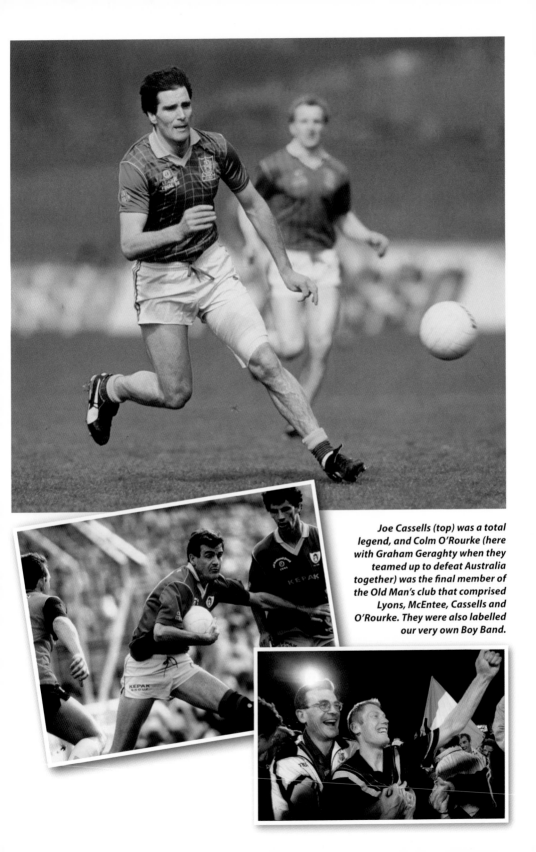

Joe Cassells (top) was a total legend, and Colm O'Rourke (here with Graham Geraghty when they teamed up to defeat Australia together) was the final member of the Old Man's club that comprised Lyons, McEntee, Cassells and O'Rourke. They were also labelled our very own Boy Band.

Nobody put the fear of God into opposing forwards in our defence more than Liam Harnan, but it was Colm Coyle (below) who I soldiered with longest as we became the two elder statesmen on the team that won the All-Ireland in 1996.

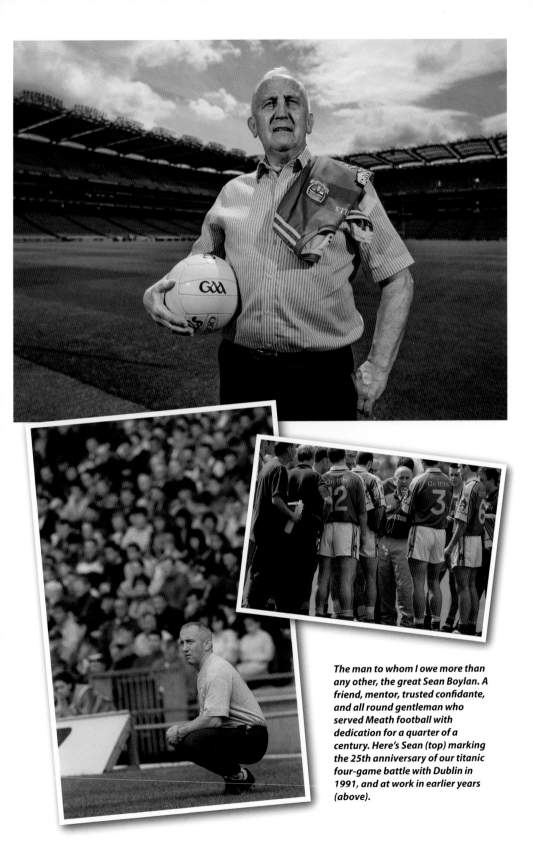

The man to whom I owe more than any other, the great Sean Boylan. A friend, mentor, trusted confidante, and all round gentleman who served Meath football with dedication for a quarter of a century. Here's Sean (top) marking the 25th anniversary of our titanic four-game battle with Dublin in 1991, and at work in earlier years (above).

My career went by too fast. It was amazing and more than I ever imagined, and I certainly did not think I would be honoured by the GAA in getting chosen for the left half-back position on the Team of the Millennium (below) when a postage stamp was issued with my face on it. Imagine that!

some reason. It was a really flat game. Colm O'Neill got sent off for punching Mick – that famous moment when Mick just held his jaw and walked away. When Paddy Russell sent him off, I remember thinking, *We're definitely going to win this now.*

It was a dreadful game. I think only two or three of us played well. I thought I did okay, and Terry Ferguson did well. We had a couple of good goal chances that we didn't take. Our whole performance was very dead. We just couldn't get going at all. Maybe there were mistakes made on the line. I remember Mick was inside in the full-back line all on his own because his man had been sent off, and he was doing absolutely nothing.

I said to him at one stage when things weren't going well, 'Mick, you go out and I'll hang in around here'. But we got no instructions from the line to tell Mick to go out, and we were probably half-afraid to make changes ourselves.

Looking back on it, we probably should have. That's no disrespect to the selectors, it was just one of those things and, in fairness to Sean, he might have been thinking that if he moved Mick out and left things open at the back, maybe Cork would get in for a goal.

I don't think we reacted to the sending off quickly enough. The irony was that we were so used to playing with a man down ourselves over the years, but we didn't know what to do when we had the extra man.

I always maintain that the problem that day was we didn't know who the spare man was. Colm Coyle was the spare man for a while when he came on at half-time, but I was running around at different stages with nobody near me, and Mick was spare for a while. Even to this day at club level, if an opposition player gets sent off, a bit of panic sets in, because you don't know where best to put the extra man.

In hindsight, it's good to expect the unexpected and be ready for what might happen. I don't think we were ready for what happened that day. The spare man should always be around the middle of the field, in my opinion. That's where a lot of the play is going to be, especially at that time when virtually all the kick-outs went long. Goalkeepers then would have been afraid to go short in case they were caught out. We weren't prepared for it. We were a bit confused, and I think that's what cost us.

We were a little bit too relaxed, too casual. Bernard Flynn kicked a free wide off his hands in the first-half which would always have been put on the floor for Stafford to hit. I could be blamed, too, because Shay Fahy kicked four points that day. Now Shay, I hope he doesn't mind me saying it, but he normally wouldn't score if the goals were on wheels!

But I gifted him two points that day, because I kicked two balls straight to him and he turned and put them straight over the bar. So I gave him two points and we were beaten by two. It does come back to haunt me sometimes when I think about that All-Ireland final, because I kicked those two balls straight down his throat and he stuck them over. But definitely, I think the word to sum up that game from our perspective is casual. I think we were cock-sure we were going to win.

I don't really remember the pre-match team-talk or anything that day. Maybe the games you lose you just erase from the memory! But we would have approached it the same as we would have approached any other big match. It was just that we'd played Cork so often and got the better of them each time, so we were very confident of winning.

Some people were surprised that Tommy Dowd was dropped for that final. Gerry Mc came back in at midfield and Colm Brady was switched to wing-forward. Cork were very strong around the middle, so maybe that was in Sean's mind. But Tommy had done fairly well in the Leinster final, and in the semi-final too, so it was tough on him to be dropped. But that game was very disappointing for everyone.

At half-time, I was sure we were going to win as we were only one down. The longer the second-half went on though, the more I started to think it wasn't going to be our day. Cork seemed to be getting all the breaks, and John Kerins made a great save from Stafford after Liam Hayes had made one of his trademark runs down the middle. On another day, that goes in and you win.

Having the extra man definitely put pressure on us. In the replay in 1988, we were so determined because Cork had knocked the shite out of us the first day. So even when we went a man down, we didn't lose focus. But for some reason in 1990, we did. I don't think Cork were that much better than us. I think we were a better team man-for-man, though I would say that.

We didn't convert our chances, we panicked, we lost our way... and it was very hard to find our way back. We were experienced enough to get it back, but tactics, gameplans... everything went out the window.

The game just flew by, and we lost by two in the end.

IN HINDSIGHT, MAYBE we'd have been better off if Mick had been sent off along with Colm O'Neill. Mick always said that – that he should have got up, hit O'Neill a box, the two of them would have been sent off and it would have been 14 vs 14.

I blame myself for losing that game in some ways, and Mick would be the same. Even now he says, 'I should have clocked him'.

That level of restraint wouldn't have been like Mick, either. If you gave him a box like that in training, you'd get about 10 back! I know if it was Harnan or Foley, all hell would have broken loose. If you were putting money on it, you'd say... Mick will retaliate here, but for some reason, something stopped him. Maybe if it was 14 on 14, everyone would have been on a man and panic wouldn't have set in, but hindsight's a great thing.

Harnan was injured that year and he was a huge loss, because if you look at a lot of the Cork scores that day, they came down the middle. If Harnan was there, they mightn't just have got those scores as easily. The common theme from all the Leinster or All-Ireland finals that we lost is that there were really central, pivotal players missing in each of those game.

Mick in 1984 and '89.

Harnan in 1990.

Bob and Colm in 1991.

That's not taking away from the teams that beat us, that's just how it went. It just shows how reliant we were on certain fellas.

Aside from the sending off, there wasn't a lot of needle in that 1990 final, which I found strange, given how the previous games between Meath and Cork had gone. There was always a bit of aggravation, always a bit of tension. That was completely missing this time around. It was just a flat game and a flat performance from us. Our attitude wasn't right, and we paid the price.

AT THE TAIL-END of 1990, Ireland travelled to Australia for the International Rules series. Eugene McGee, who sadly passed away early in 2019, was the manager and he invited me in to the training panel in the month or so before the squad flew out. The training was really tough – I'd say even tougher than what Sean did with us.

We'd play games which were, naturally enough, divided up into quarters. So we'd go 100 miles an hour for 15 or 20 minutes, then take a break, then go again. It was my first time training at that level with someone other than Sean, so it was interesting to see how someone else worked. Eugene was very similar to Sean in a lot of ways, too. He was very professional, maybe even more so because this was Ireland we were going to be representing.

Unfortunately, in the end I had to tell him that I couldn't go. I had started up my own business at that stage and there was no way I could afford to be away for three weeks. I regretted it in many ways, but there was no way around it.

Bob and Bernard Flynn went and had a brilliant time. I nearly didn't want to talk to them when they came back because I didn't want to hear about all the craic that I'd missed out on! Bob was captain and Ireland won the series 2-1, so it was a fantastic honour for him, and something that I know he was really proud of.

If there was any way I could have gone, I'd have been first on the plane. It was maybe the first time in my life that football came second, but sometimes it has to.

CHAPTER 12

FRIDAY, MAY 17, 1991

THE YEAR 1991 saw the arrival of sponsorship.

The year that the names of sponsors were first allowed on GAA shirts. Noel Keating from Kepak was always in the background in Meath and he always looked after us even before sponsorship officially came in. He didn't really get involved with the county board, he was more concerned with the players, and he looked after us really well.

He's not with us anymore sadly. He died a young man and he was a huge loss to everybody, and not just his family. Noel used to sort us out with a few steaks and a few other bits and pieces. People talk about dieticians these days, but we used to go down to Bellinter – where the Bellinter House Hotel is now – and we'd have steak, and it could be half nine at night. It didn't do us any harm, and in spite of what some people would have you believe, none of us ate it raw!

THAT PARTICULAR YEAR, I was after breaking two bones in my shoulder with my club, and I was out for six weeks. I was only back training for two weeks when we played a challenge match against Galway in Summerhill.

I got two of the best wallops you'd ever get, and I knew then that I was right. I would have been a bit apprehensive after getting an injury, but I got these two belts – one after another – and there wasn't a bother on me. That gave me the confidence to go full-tilt again.

But I ran out of legs in that game, and I was taken off near the end. I was banjaxed! I would never put my hand up to Sean to sub me, but I'd say he saw me looking over at him and took me off.

Another first that year was that the GAA held open draws in the provincial championships and, who did we get... Dublin.

Meeting Dublin in the first round would have been something totally new for us. I remember the draw being made at the back end of 1990. From that moment on, even when we were going out playing league games, Dublin was on everyone's minds – and we were still six months away from the game. We were so used to meeting in a Leinster final, so to be meeting in a first round game was going to be huge.

Little did any of us know just how huge it was going to be.

Sean was very good at keeping us grounded and keeping us right. We would have been as fit for that first round game as we would have been for a Leinster final, which wouldn't have been the norm for us. Generally we'd be fit enough, but we'd build up the fitness levels as we went through Leinster. This time, however, we all knew we'd have to be incredibly fit to play Dublin. When we did eventually get through those games, we eased back a little. When it came to judging what training was needed and when, there was nobody better than Sean Boylan.

'We'll have you right for this game,' he'd always tell us.

And, he had us right pretty much all the time. He was well able to put the pressure on in training, but he would also ease it off when he needed to.

The first game against Dublin was nip and tuck, as they all turned out to be. They were leading by one with time almost up, and Mick Deegan burst out with the ball. He probably should have kicked it into Row Z, but he got caught under the Hogan Stand by David Beggy, who just got a hand in.

It popped up for PJ Gillic. And PJ sent it in towards the goal.

It could have hopped into the net, or it could have hopped wide, but it hopped over the bar. We were after coming back from being a few points behind, so we were happy enough to take a draw.

The training in between those games wasn't overly heavy. You couldn't really do much with the games coming so thick and fast, so we were just tipping away. We were after training so hard in the lead-up to that first round because it was Dublin. We'd have games between ourselves, and we talked about what we did right or wrong.

Training itself was light enough. The Tuesday after the game we'd do very little, the Thursday might be a bit tougher, then on the Saturday or Sunday we'd be on the field kicking a few balls, just keeping an eye in and keeping fresh as much as anything. Sean always had that knack for keeping fellas fresh.

THAT YEAR, AS with every time we met, it was a battle of wills against Dublin. Tactics went out the window.

You could sit and talk for half an hour about what you were going to do, but as soon as the ball was thrown in, it all went out the window, and Dublin would probably say the same. It was every man for himself. There was no need for pep-talks or psyching anyone up – the sight of the blue jersey did that. It was very easy to get yourself 'up' for playing Dublin. But tactics weren't much of a feature in those games.

The second game, we got out of jail there a bit, too.

Vinny Murphy had a great chance at the end. A high ball came in and I ended up back in the full-back line for some reason. Vinny pushed me in the back. He was cute because the referee was running straight up the field so all he could see was me – he couldn't see Vinny behind me. So he gave me a nudge, and he was in.

He went for a goal, and Mickey McQuillan came out and saved it. If he had fisted it over the bar, the game was over. But justice was done, because Vinny got away with a push! It reminded me a bit of Seamus Darby's goal in 1982 against Kerry – just a little nudge to ease me out of the way.

I was working for myself at that stage, and those games quickly became the talk of the country, never mind the county. I was going in to meet customers, and everyone wanted to talk about Meath and Dublin.

I couldn't give them the deaf ear and not talk to them. Everyone meant well and all that but my God, it would get to you. It made me think of Harnan down the fields again. I was in the public eye because I was in my van driving around, and going into shops in Navan, Kells, Dublin – I was all over the place. If I had a pound for every time it was mentioned, I'd be a millionaire.

Looking back on it now, it was great, but at the time it was tough. I wanted to forget about it, because I was talking about it day and night. I was listening to Sean talking about it at training in the evening, then getting up in the morning to go to work and the same thing, over… and over and over. I could nearly have taped my answers and just handed people the recording, and then go about my business.

I was just saying the same thing to everybody I met.

I wasn't the only one. Mick Lyons had it in the shop, and some of the lads were in sales rep jobs, so they'd all have to put up with a bit of it. I had my name on the van in green and gold – that's what I signed up for, you have to take the good with the bad!

I was at midfield for the third game, which wouldn't have been somewhere I'd have played too often for Meath, though I played there for the club. Sean had put me there a few times in training before that game, so I had a fair idea he was planning it. Liam Hayes was there and he hadn't been changed. He had three different partners in midfield over the four games. I think some people were wondering why Liam wasn't dropped, but he was captain that year and he hung in there! It didn't bother me where I played, because after walking away in 1987, I said when I came back that I'd play wherever they put me.

Once again, Dublin looked to be home and dry that day. They were ahead by five points with 10 minutes left, and Colm Coyle put a ball in that Bernard Flynn punched into the net – it was really brave from Bernie to get to that ball. We weren't playing well, but that goal got us back into it, and we got a couple of points to get the draw.

Into extra-time we went, and Coyler got a goal right from the throw-in, but we conceded a goal almost immediately. Lads were getting tired at that stage, on both sides. In the second half of extra-time, there were only a couple of points scored by each side. Everyone was out on their feet.

Dublin missed a couple of great chances to win it at the end. I remember Paul Clarke shooting from about 40 metres with one of the last kicks of the game, when he had Vinny Murphy totally free inside. But between the exhaustion and the tension a lot of mistakes were made on both sides.

Dublin probably felt they should have won it again, while we were happy once again to get another shot at it. We were probably blessed that we didn't lose three of the four games when you look back at it now.

On the weekend between the third and fourth games, we went away. We didn't know a thing about it until the day before. We trained on the Tuesday night as usual, then after training on Thursday Sean said that he wanted everyone up in Dublin airport at four o'clock on the Friday afternoon.

He just told us that we were going away for the weekend, and we were just told to pack a bag. We had no idea where we were going.

Not a clue. Wives, girlfriends, everyone was coming. I went home and packed, landed at the airport the following day, and found out we were going to a place called Drymen in Scotland. David Beggy was working over in Scotland at the time, and I think he recommended it. We found out later that Sean and Noel Keating had gone out the previous Monday and sussed this place out. It was only a small little village – it wouldn't be the size of Kilmessan or Carlanstown.

There was a pub, a hotel, and a few shops in it. We arrived over, checked in, and came down for a bite to eat. After we had eaten, Sean told us to enjoy ourselves – and, by God, did we enjoy ourselves!

We had a great night. There was no expense spared, and that was where Noel Keating came in – he looked after everybody. We drank and we chatted until all hours. It was a great bonding session. Lads stayed out half the night.

There was the hotel in one corner of the village, and a pub in the other. In the middle was this little green. The next morning, there were stools and chairs and benches on the green. I think one or two lads even slept on the benches! I'd say the villagers didn't know what was going on.

We trained the next morning at 11 o'clock, and we were dying – I mean dying! There was a little soccer pitch that was about a mile or so from the village, so we used that.

Sean started us off, and we had to do a couple of laps.

We ran around the back of this little cabin at the side of the pitch as we went. On the second or third lap, half of us stopped on the far side of the cabin where Sean couldn't see us, and puked our guts up.

Then we got going again.

It was amazing how much better you'd feel after being sick! In the meantime, Mochie Regan was bringing water from the hotel over to us. The people in the village thought we were mad. We trained, felt great afterwards, had a bit of a chat, then did the same thing on the Saturday night – had a few drinks.

On the Sunday morning we trained again. Nobody got sick this time! We played a game and knocked the shite out of one another, had a few arguments, cleared the air. And that was it.

It was a great idea for Sean to bring us to Scotland, because it took us away from the limelight back home, even if it was only for two days. It was certainly a break for me, because I was talking about it every day of the week, no more than a lot of the lads. Nobody over there knew who we were, although they certainly knew after it!

It would be unheard of now to do something like that the week before a big game, but it got us out of the bubble and we could let off a bit of steam. It probably brought its own pressure in some ways, because people knew we'd gone away and had a great time, so if we'd lost you could say it had backfired.

People would have been asking why we went away, why were we drinking and so on? Fortunately, everything fell into place.

As had happened in each of the first three games, things didn't get off to the best of starts for us in the fourth game – the third replay. Before we even got onto the pitch, we had lost two players. Sean Kelly failed a late fitness test and, when we were getting togged out in the dressing-room, Terry Ferguson pulled a muscle in his back. He was sitting next to me, and bent down to take off his trousers. Next thing, poor Terry is locked in that position and can't move.

So that was him gone. Pádraig Lyons started in Terry's place, but then *he* got injured shortly after the game started. Things were going completely against us.

With the game not long on, Colm got an unmerciful belt off Eamonn Heery and Keith Barr. Brian Stafford gave him a hospital pass, and O'Rourke got caught between the two lads and was creased. There were are few body-blows in the space of 10 or 15 minutes and I was thinking... *This isn't going to be our day.*

I also thought about how we'd been drinking in Scotland – having a great time – and now here we were, struggling. Colm went off for a few minutes but somehow recovered and we pulled ourselves back into it.

Staff was on form with his frees, as usual, and that kept us in touch. We went in two behind at half-time, but Dublin pulled away a bit in the second-half and led by six points with about 20 minutes to go.

We had been up against it at different stages of the other games but, this time, I really thought we were done. Even when Staff got a goal to pull it back to two points, Dublin kicked on again.

They then got a penalty, which would absolutely have finished it, but Keith Barr drove it wide. I know, at the time, people were saying that it should have been retaken because Mick Lyons nearly got to the ball before Barr, but neither Dublin nor Keith himself ever complained about that. In fact, I think Barr said he never even noticed Mick – he was more concerned with the 20,000 Meath fans on the Canal End!

The penalty miss was a lifeline, but we were being beaten all over the field. It was probably the worst game of football I ever played for Meath. I think I got one ball into my hands all day, and that was the ball I stopped from going out over the end-line that eventually led to the goal. We just couldn't get going, especially in the second-half.

Everything seemed to be going against us. Dublin were on a roll, they seemed to be fitter than us, and Niall Guiden was flying. It was a scorching hot day – the heat was unbelievable – and any changes we could have made were impacted by losing Terry and Sean before the game, and then Pádraig going off early.

But we never gave up, we kept chipping away. It just felt like we had run out of road. Little things were going against us and against me. I came onto a few breaking balls around the middle, and I'd think I had it, then someone would get a hand in and knock it away. Colm Coyle let a roar at me.

'LEAVE IT!'

Whatever way it bounced, it went over his head and he gave a free away. Things really weren't going well at all, but that can happen in games.

The never-say-die attitude was something that became a hallmark of that Meath team and people would often wonder where it came from. There was no big secret to it, really. Firstly, Sean drilled it into us that you never give up, ever. Along with that, there were big characters on the team who would have had that attitude anyway.

One little bit of advice Sean would give us was to watch the clock. There used to be a clock up on the Canal End, and Sean would always, 'Keep an eye on the clock', especially if there was maybe three or four minutes to half-time – that was the time to kick on. I'd always take a quick look up during a game to see what was left. But really, it was just drilled into us that you never gave up, and I think a lot of teams after us that won All-Irelands – like Armagh, for example – brought that attitude with them, too.

Even to this day when I'm coaching teams, I always let them know that it's never over until it's over. All of that being said, it did look like we were down and out against Dublin that day. But we just kept going and going. Where it took us that day was within three points – striking distance – of Dublin with time almost up.

We really had no right to be that close.

And then…

IT STARTED WITH me, and it was a ball I should never have got. Paul Curran drop-kicked it from his own half-back line, and it ended up with Vinny Murphy.

Bob O'Malley was coming thundering towards Vinny and he flicked the ball quickly to his left in the direction of Declan Sheehan. It went beyond Declan towards the end-line, and I just happened to be there.

I shouldn't have been back there.

But, I stopped the ball going out. My feet were out, but the ball wasn't. I turned and fell forwards, but as I fell, I hand-passed it to Mick Lyons. Sheehan should have put me out over the end-line by fair means or foul, and I'm sure the Dublin lads told him that after! Fortunately for me, he didn't.

Mick got it and took a heavy knock from Vinny Murphy, but he got the elbow up just in time and rode that challenge, before dinking one up the line to Mattie McCabe, who flicked it into Harnan.

Harnan played a very dribbly pass – he'll love me for saying that – into O'Rourke. Colm was fouled around half-way and took a quick free. It was the worst pass you'd ever see – about 20 yards behind David Beggy under the Hogan Stand.

Beggy scrambled back and picked it up, took a couple of solos, and hand-passed it in to Foley. Foley passed it on to PJ Gillic, and after he gave the pass, I remember looking at him making a bee-line towards the goals. In the meantime, PJ had given it to Tommy Dowd, Tommy played a one-two with O'Rourke, gave it to Foley and… BANG!!!!

Back of the net.

I'm not sure what was more incredible – the fact that we'd gotten the goal or the fact that Foley had got it.

SEAN HAD US carrying the ball in training to try to work a goal, but I couldn't say that it ever went quite like it did in that game, because there were a few hairy passes along the way! I looked back on it on television soon after, and I noticed Keith Barr was really struggling to get back, he was just jogging back.

That wouldn't be like Keith. He was out on his feet. Dublin were just cut open and it was like they didn't even have the energy to take a fella out.

Ordinarily, the Tommy Dowd give-and-go would never be let happen – he'd have been taken out. Looking back at the goal on TV, you could maybe see it coming, but maybe that's because you know it's coming. During the game, I didn't see it happening until the ball came to Foley. We got that bit of energy from somewhere, we knew it was the last throw of the dice. When Tommy got it, he injected that bit of pace.

I was barely after getting back off the ground when the goal went in! But the crowd went mad, and Mick was beside me, with Harnan and Bob… and we all got this new energy into us.

We started shouting to each other.

'WE HAVE IT!'

That wasn't happening 10 minutes earlier, because we thought we were dead and buried. It's amazing the effect a score like that can have.

Even with the goal though, we were only back on level terms, so it was looking like another 20 minutes of extra-time. John O'Leary kicked the ball out, and Mattie McCabe caught it. You don't see that on the TV footage, so poor Mattie doesn't get the credit for it!

He passed it on to Hayes, who soloed in and popped it over to PJ.

Eamonn Heery tried to close PJ down, but he was exhausted, and the ball was played over his head to his man, David Beggy. Now Beggy, from a standing position, wouldn't be the most accurate fella. He could kick a point from the corner flag, but in front of the goals - he'd tell you himself - it could go anywhere.

Luckily enough on this occasion, it went over the bar. Mick O'Dwyer, on commentary, said it was Flynn, but that just showed you how excited everyone was getting, including the commentators. Dublin should have put us away, but they left us in the game.

They got one last chance. Jack Sheedy had a free from about 60 metres. He had the distance, and he hit it a fair belt, but it went wide. The ball was kicked out, and that was it.

All over. We had somehow pulled it out.

I don't think too many of us were jumping around when the final whistle went. It was more a feeling of relief, and a little bit of shock.

How did we win this game?

We were playing so badly. Dublin were performing much better than us and they were always ahead. So it was pure relief more than anything else. There was an air of silence on Hill 16.

No-one left the Hill for a while, they were just stunned. Meanwhile, the

Meath fans were going mad. I don't think the players went overboard on the celebrating, because there was great respect there. Nobody rubbed it in. I swapped jerseys with Declan Sheehan, and walked off with Kieran Duff and we had a bit of a chat. It wasn't like after you'd won an All-Ireland or a Leinster.

I felt sorry for Dublin because they were after putting in a huge effort, and the way they got beaten... it wouldn't have been nice if it had happened to us. But they took it on the chin, and wished us all the best. That was the character of that Dublin team.

There was great respect on both sides.

Back in the dressing-room, it was much the same, nobody was going too mad. It was more a case of lads shaking hands and congratulating each other. We'd won nothing yet – it was only the first round of the championship, after all – and we were out the following Sunday against Wicklow. After the game, we were brought to the Mansion House for a reception that the Lord Mayor of Dublin had organised. A lot of lads weren't too keen on that, it might have been better to do it later in the year when the dust had settled. We had a couple of drinks in the Skylon Hotel, then headed up to the Mansion House.

Liam Hayes got up and said a few words, but he kept it very short and sweet. Tommy Carr got up and he spoke for a while, it had obviously hit him hard. It was just devastating for the Dublin lads, they couldn't believe it.

We had a bite to eat, but we couldn't really wait to get out of there. I'd say Dublin felt the same. It wasn't something we were overly keen on attending, but we were invited, so it was only good manners to go. Even to this day, if we're asked to do something – the bond we have with a lot of those Dublin lads – we'll do it.

But I don't think it was the right time for something like that straight after the game, particularly for the Dublin lads. We had all seen enough of each other at that stage. The saga was finally over, and we were the ones left standing.

Just.

CHAPTER **13**

GUARANTEED: 48,000 US VISAS

"Irish citizens interested in working legally in the United States can now avail of the 48,000 immigrant visas which have been recently allocated to Irish Nationals under the AA-1 (Morrisson) Immigration Act 1990. Ireland is the only country to get a guaranteed share of the total 120,000 Green Cards. The Act enables undocumented Irish citizens working in the United States and Irish residents here in Ireland to gain legal status in the US."

MEATH TAKE SCENIC ROUTE
Meath 1-9 Wicklow 0-12

"This, of course, is the year of draws in Gaelic Games competition, but nobody really expected this Leinster Football Championship quarter-final to end in stalemate. However, no-hopers Wicklow bravely defied all the odds at Croke Park yesterday against mighty Meath and the two counties have to return to Headquarters next Sunday to decide who will provide the opposition to Offaly in the Leinster semi-final. The Royal County seemed to have clinched a penultimate place when sub Bernard Flynn kicked a point. But referee Noel Whelan ruled that he had blown the final whistle before Flynn kicked the ball, so the 'score' was not allowed."

The Irish Independent

AFTER COMING THROUGH the four-game saga with Dublin, it was very difficult to lift ourselves for Wicklow. No disrespect to them, but we had been looking forward to the Dublin match for six months, and then it took four games to get over them.

All of a sudden, we're back out eight days later.

So of course it was very hard to motivate ourselves after what we'd been through against Dublin. Sean and the management team warned us not to take Wicklow for granted. They had seen us four times, and they knew where we were weak and where we were strong. But even with that, it was still hard to motivate ourselves. We underestimated Wicklow, which was easy to do after all the hullabaloo with the Dublin games.

I was corner-back, and I ended up marking Kevin O'Brien, because he moved out from full-forward onto me – probably hoping Mick would follow him.

We were under serious pressure in that game, and it was level with time almost up. Right at the end, Bernard Flynn got a ball, turned his man and put it straight over the bar. But as the ball was in flight, the referee blew the final whistle. I was standing right behind it, and it went straight over the black spot. I couldn't believe that the ref blew up.

Even with all the noise in Croke Park I heard him blowing, so I knew he wasn't going to allow it. Another draw – just what we needed!

WICKLOW HAD A really good team at that time, so we shouldn't have taken them so lightly. Kevin O'Brien was one of the best forwards in the country, and he was probably one of the toughest opponents I've had to mark.

He played in the International Rules series for Ireland and would have got his place on any team in the land. They had two top midfielders in Pat O'Byrne and Fergus Daly. O'Byrne was a sheep farmer and was a hardy bit of stuff; he played for Ireland against Australia aswell. So they had a really useful team, and we got out of jail, even allowing for that point at the end that wasn't given. But I would say it was all down to a lack of motivation, and struggling to boost ourselves after playing Dublin four times.

We beat them by three points in the replay. Liam Hayes was sent off, as was Hugh Kenny after he was involved in an incident with Bernard Flynn. There was a little bit of needle in both of those games, they knew what we were all about and got stuck into us. In the replay, we were better prepared and we knew what to expect. The following year, Bernard was playing for Mullingar Shamrocks against Baltinglass and he picked up a really bad knee injury – he snapped every ligament going. I remember we had been training a few days before he played that game, and I had said to him to be careful. I always felt that if you're a big name and you're playing with a club outside of your home county, you're going to be targeted. So it was just unfortunate that he got that injury, because it was a bad one and kept him out for a long time.

We got over Offaly handy enough in the semi-final, then it was on to Laois in the Leinster final. We lost Bob early in that game, which was a huge blow to us. He clashed with Mick Lyons, and broke his leg. Flynn's man, Tommy Smith, got sent off just after David Beggy got our goal. This was a recurring theme now, so I don't know if the problem was Flynn or the lads he was marking!

I got Man of the Match that day. I got an engraved watch for it. It was great to finally get some silverware. It had taken us eight games to win a Leinster and we were into August. That Leinster final was played the day before the first All-Ireland semi-final, in which Down beat Kerry. It was just bang, bang… BANG!

Game after game. We probably fancied ourselves to win a Leinster once we got over Dublin, but we didn't think it'd take two games to get over Wicklow. We were constantly going, but the positive thing was that there was very little training done – Sean knew how to keep us ticking over.

After winning Leinster, we were out eight days later in the All-Ireland semi-final against Roscommon – another one that went down to the wire. We were behind for pretty much all of that game. Brian Stafford got the last few points for us to win it by one. It was a really hot day, and I was marking Junior McManus. They also had Tony McManus, Paul Earley and Derek Duggan, who was only a young lad at the time. He had scored a massive free in the Connacht final, so was getting rave reviews.

We started fairly slowly, and Roscommon went a few points up. We couldn't get into it at all, but we were fortunate that they missed an awful lot of scores early on, including a few goal chances. We could have been six or seven down at half-time. Just before the break, Duggan got a ball inside and he sold Terry Ferguson down the river with a dummy. Poor Terry was trying to get back to block the shot, and Duggan just dummy-soloed it. Terry bought the dummy and went flying, and Duggan dropped-kicked it into the bottom corner. It was a brilliant finish in fairness to him. We went in three behind.

In the dressing-room at half-time, Sean made a few changes. I went in corner-back on Duggan. Thankfully, things went my way in the second-half and he didn't get too much ball. But they had us in trouble and we had to move things around a bit. With 65 minutes gone, Roscommon were still winning.

We got a few frees and Brian knocked them over, and he got a point or two from play. We only took the lead for the first time in the dying minutes, and scraped through by a point. Meath fans probably would have expected us to win that game fairly easily, but when you look through the footballers that Roscommon had, they were a really good team.

THERE HAD BEEN so many times that year where it looked like we were dead and buried, and we managed to come back.

We never panicked. Obviously, Keith Barr should have finished us with the penalty in the fourth game against Dublin, and then we had the battles with Wicklow. The only easy game we had all year was against Offaly in the Leinster semi-final. So when we came from behind against Roscommon, maybe we thought that no matter how far behind we were, we'd always come back.

That wasn't the way to be thinking when you look at what happened in the final.

The month gap to the All-Ireland final was the worst thing that ever happened. We were on a bit of a roll, and I think if the All-Ireland final had been two weeks later, it would have been better. We didn't know what to do with ourselves. It was back to training, and back meeting people on the streets again.

We were in a routine for the whole summer of playing games week in, week out. Then all of a sudden it was broken, and we had a month of a wait until the next game.

On the other side of it, we thought we might have Bob back for the final. He did absolutely everything in his power to get back. He was on the bike, he was in the gym, then he tried running, but the game came a few weeks too soon for him. It had only been five weeks since he'd had the injury, so it was just devastating for him and everyone else that he wasn't back, because he was a huge loss. Not alone was Bob the best corner-back in Meath, I thought he was the best corner-back in the country. I'd go as far as saying he was the best I've ever seen. He was a superb player.

So, the month gap was good in terms of giving Bob as much time as possible to get back but, overall, if you asked any of the lads, they'd have preferred it if the final came two weeks earlier. We wouldn't have had Bob, but we would have had Colm O'Rourke, who got sick the week of the final. It was swings and roundabouts. These things happen, but we seemed to have a run of really bad luck in those few years when it came to big players missing big games.

It's easy saying it now, but I thought we'd take Down. They had beaten Kerry comfortably enough in the semi-final, but I think if Kerry had made it through, we'd have been more on our guard – simply because it was Kerry. Maybe we underestimated Down a bit.

They had brilliant forwards, but I don't think their backs were as good a unit as some other teams we'd have faced. Pete McGrath and his selectors had their homework done on us. I was playing wing half-back, and they would suck me in tight to Harnan, and the same with Foley on the far side. Their two half-forwards tucked right in, and then there was space for Mickey Linden and James McCartan in the corners. If we had only stayed out wider, we'd have been able to cut off the supply, but hindsight is a great thing.

I spoke to Ross Carr, who I was marking in that final, a few years back and he said as much. They watched us and they knew that once they got in behind Harnan, that they'd be able to spread the ball around. They had spotted a weakness you could say.

We'd have been known as a very strong half-back line – Foley, Harnan and myself – but they got around us. People might be surprised to hear that we were pulled in so easily, given how experienced we were. But back then, you just stuck with your man, and maybe we didn't cop on to what was happening. I spent most of my time that day more towards the centre, when I should have been out wide.

Maybe we should have realised ourselves what was going on, but when you're out there and the crowd is roaring and you're looking to see where your man it, it's not always easy to see things clearly. If you left your man and he started getting a lot of ball, you'd be in trouble then, too.

The funny thing about that game was it was the first one all year where we got off to a flying start. We got the first two points of the game inside the opening couple of minutes. Even at that stage I thought to myself... *This is going to be our day.*

But it wasn't long before it all got turned on its head.

Down really got into the game and were up 0-8 to 0-4 at half-time. In spite of that, the mood in the dressing-room was fairly good. We hadn't played that well in the first-half and we knew we'd have to up it a good bit, but I felt good. We knew we were in a battle, and you never like to be behind at half-time, but I still felt like we were going to win it.

By the fifteenth minute of the second half, we were 11 points (1-14 to 0-6) behind. Everything was going against us. Mick Lyons was in trouble at that stage, he came back out after half-time with a knee bandage on, and for Down's goal, Mickey Linden side-stepped Mick easily and squared it to Barry Breen, who palmed it to the net. Mick's knee was gone, so there was nothing he could do.

I had been watching Ross Carr, but I saw Breen drifting in towards goal.

I better follow this fella.

But I couldn't get there in time. If you look at the footage, I'm getting there, but I was two or three seconds too late.

The damage was done in the opening quarter of that second-half, and that coincided with Mick carrying the knee. He eventually went off. Maybe he should have been taken off at half-time, but Mick would always want to play on if he could at all.

When that ball hit the net, that's when I knew we were in real trouble. This might be asking for one miracle too many. But O'Rourke came on – he had had pneumonia all week and didn't start – and the crowd got behind us. Liam Hayes got a great goal, and Bernard kicked some brilliant scores – he got six points that day, three off his left, three off his right. He's probably haunted by the goal chance he had which Neil Collins saved.

So even though we were 11 down at one stage, we had enough chances to win it. We chased them down, and the referee blew it up a bit early, I think. If we'd had another couple of minutes, we would have caught them, because you could see the Down players were panicking a bit. Their supporters on the Hill had gone quiet, and their players were asking how long was left, which is always a sign of panic in my book.

It's still a bitter one to take, even to this day. I'd be telling lies if I said otherwise.

WHEN THE FINAL whistle went, I dropped to my hunkers and I cried.

It was the first time I had cried after a game. It was a feeling of pure devastation. When we got back to two points, I really thought we were going to win.

All of a sudden, the final whistle went.

I was in a state of shock for a few moments, then I saw all the Down lads celebrating. After that, it's all a bit of a blur. Someone from Down came into our dressing-room – possibly Paddy O'Rourke and Pete McGrath – I'm not sure.

The difference a couple of years makes. To win two in-a-row in 1987 and '88 was unreal. Then to get to two more… to get to the All-Ireland final in 1990, and lose it. Then another one in '91, and lose that, too – 1991 actually felt like losing two All-Irelands in one year. That's how hard it was to take.

In 1990, we didn't play that well, so you could probably accept that one. But in '91, to have jumped nine fences and fall at the last… it was a sickening blow. I knew then how Cork felt in 1987 and '88, but at least they came back and won in 1989 and '90.

The day after, we went to the winners' hotel for a bit of a function. I think Down were in The Burlington. When we walked in, we got a standing ovation from the Down players and supporters.

That was a really nice touch, and we got great credit from people all over the country for our efforts that year. We got respect that we maybe hadn't always had. The irony was that we got slated in 1988 when we won it, and then it all turned around three years later when we had been beaten. I suppose a lot of that was down to the 10 games and the way we conducted ourselves.

There was no animosity towards Down, we wished them all the best. It was great to get that respect after what had been written and said after the 1988 All-Ireland. Of course, you'd still rather win and get criticised, than lose and get praised.

I'd still see a bit of Ross Carr and Mickey Linden – St Michael's put on a *'This Is Your Life'* thing for me and they came down for it – and they'd know how tough that defeat was to take. It was like a death when that final whistle went.

We bankrupted the Meath supporters that year with all the games, but the night after the Down game, you'd think we had won it with the reception we got.

The crowds were huge. All that was missing was the Sam Maguire.

IT TURNED OUT to be the end of an era, but at the time I didn't think of it that way. I thought we'd come back and go again the following year, because losing an All-Ireland wasn't the way that team would have wanted to bow out.

I didn't get the feeling from anyone that they were planning to give it up. It was hard to get back into it for the league, but once you get back to training and get your first league game over with, it's a new season and you're away again. You get over defeats. That one just took a little bit longer than most.

I got married in October 1991, three weeks after that All-Ireland final. I delayed my wedding because of the football.

Football always came first.

So myself and Samantha tied the knot in October. I thought I was going to have two Sams at the wedding! I had Samantha Kearney, but sadly no Sam Maguire. It would have been nice, because I think Terry Ferguson got married one of the years we won it, and had 'Sam' at the reception.

I wanted the two Sams, but I better not say I'd have preferred Sam Maguire or I'll be in trouble! I think the headline in the paper the next day was…

GOODBYE SAM, HELLO SAMANTHA

We always put football first, so that was why we got married in October. Nowadays, I don't think it would happen as much!

As I had expected, pretty much everyone was back for another crack at it in 1992. Gerry Mc had retired, but everyone else stuck around. We had Laois in the first round in Navan, and I was made captain for the year. I remember I was on Colm Maher, who sadly died in a fire in Portarlington back in 1996. There was a terrible accident, and he and several members of his family died. We wouldn't have met too often, but he was up in Bob O'Malley's pub one night and we had a bit of a chat. He was a nice fella, and a really good footballer. It was really tragic what happened.

Laois were hardy.

This was our third year in-a-row to meet in Leinster, so a bit of a rivalry was starting to develop, and it continued over the next few years. That 1992 game was the end of the road for a lot of that Meath team.

There were a lot of changes made to the starting 15.

Liam Hayes, Bob O'Malley and Liam Harnan were dropped. That's not to blame Sean and the selectors, because if there was ever a game that we thought we were going to win, it was Laois in Navan in the first round. Maybe they thought they could afford to give a few new lads a go.

Alan Browne was at centre-back, Enda McManus at corner-back and John McDermott at midfield. Laois were well up for it, and it was a game that flew by. Colm Maher was running me all over the field – he could run forever – and Leo and Mick Turley were causing us problems. Hughie Emerson was a great player, and in Barney Maher and Mick Dempsey, they had two top midfielders.

They were a fair outfit. After us beating them in the Leinster final the year before, when they probably felt hard done-by that they had a man sent off, they were really up for it. They were probably more up for it than we were. With the team we put out, with all the changes, I thought that the management took it for granted really.

While McDermott had been involved in 1991, he was still inexperienced at that level, and it probably took him another two or three years before he developed into one of the greatest midfielders Meath has ever had. He was still a bit raw going into that game in 1992, and he had to go off early on. He got a serious belt. Laois were hitting hard that day. They got a penalty late enough on and their keeper, Tony McMahon came up and scored.

That was pretty much it then. The Laois crowd came onto the field at the end and you'd think they had won the All-Ireland, which was understandable because it would have been an upset for us to lose in Navan.

WE WERE COMING out after the game, and I saw Gerry McEntee.

He wasn't involved, but he was at the game. We were devastated. With 1991 having been such a long year and such a memorable year for the most part – and really every year up until then had been fairly long – now we were gone. In May.

For the first time since 1985 we were gone really early. But we came out and there's Gerry and he smiles and said, 'Baby boom in Meath this year lads!' It lightened the mood a little bit, and it was typical Gerry. Whether there was a baby boom in Meath that year or not, I don't know! We might have to go and check the register!

Some people might have thought I'd have been glad of a shorter summer for a change, but that definitely wasn't the case. This was a big shock to me. It nearly felt worse than losing the All-Ireland the year before. To be knocked out so early, and by Laois – no disrespect to them – was hard to take, especially when you look at the changes we made. That was the end for a lot of that team. Mick went, Hayes went, McEntee was gone, and Joe Cassells was gone since 1990.

To see those lads going was a huge loss, because I respected them so much, as did everyone. We knew that, with the success of the minors and under-21s around that time, there was a core of young lads coming on. McDermott was only going to get better. McManus, Graham Geraghty, Trevor Giles… all these lads were coming through and would be the backbone of the next great team.

Sean had been there for the guts of 10 years at that stage, and I do remember there was some talk that he was going to go after that defeat. I never for a minute thought about Sean leaving. I never got tired of listening to him. I always maintain that he was way ahead of his time. A lot of what is done nowadays is what Sean did back then, only it's spoken about differently and with bigger words.

You could always go to Sean with anything, football or otherwise, and he'd always listen. He was very supportive. He's just one of those great men. Someone else coming in never entered my head. The loss of Mick and Gerry though – I would have felt that.

They had been with Meath through thick and thin before I came in, and they were a great help to me on the field and in training. They were part of the family, so when they went, I scratched my head and I missed them for a while, but then I went back training and new lads came in.

I just had to get on with it and, as a team, we had to start all over again.

CHAPTER 14

MONDAY, JULY 5, 1993

LETTER-PROMPT CLAIM AMAZES GAY

"Broadcaster Gay Byrne last night denied that people were paid to write letters to his morning show in a bid to create controversy. He told the Irish Press he was, 'astonished and amazed' that such allegations had been made and to his certain knowledge the practice of prompting letters to generate public debate on his show never took place."

SHEEDY THE DUBS HERO
Dublin 1-10 Meath 0-12

"Garda Jack Sheedy was quickest to react when Dublin sent out a distress call deep into injury-time at Croke Park yesterday. His fearless intervention prevented Meath from escaping with a share of the glory at the end of yet another absorbing tussle between two great rivals. It was fitting that Sheedy should be the man to kick the winner seventy seconds into injury-time. At the end of the epic Dublin-Meath saga in 1991, he had a chance to level the match in the third replay, but pushed a long range free just wide. Yesterday, he was on target from play from 45 metres, only this time it was the winner. Referee Tommy Howard allowed no more time, much to the delight of the Dublin fans in the crowd of 53,164."

The Irish Press

I WAS LUCKY in my career that I was rarely injured, but the worst belt I ever got happened in a National league game against Westmeath in Athlone in March, 1993. I'd say I came very close to killing myself.

I was playing centre-back, and a high ball came in.

I was backing up for it, and you're always a bit vulnerable in that situation, but I didn't get a call from anyone. The Westmeath full-forward came out from behind and pushed me into John Cooney, who was coming from in front. I was sandwiched in between the two of them. I just remember getting a bang on the head, and I fell in a heap on the ground.

Out cold.

The next thing I remember was coming around briefly in the dressing-room, because Jack Finn had the smelling salts out. Jack and Sean were there, and I was put into an ambulance. They were very concerned. I've never seen it back, and I don't ever want to see it back. It was an awful belt. It was nearly as bad as the one Colm got in the fourth game against Dublin. No cuts or anything, just a bad clash of heads.

I don't remember anything about the ambulance journey at all. I came around in Portiuncula Hospital in Ballinasloe with a nurse at my side. I felt so, so tired and I was mad to sleep, but she wouldn't let me. She kept me awake all night because I was definitely concussed. It's well-known now that if someone suffers a concussion, it's dangerous to let them sleep, but obviously it was known back then too which might surprise some people.

The next day, Samantha came down for me and brought me home, which should never have happened. I should have been kept in hospital for a few days – no doubt about it. Samantha had to stop the car five or six times on the way back to Navan because I was vomiting constantly.

I came home and went straight to bed, and I was in bed for four or five days. I lost about a stone in weight over those few days. I probably shouldn't have slept so much in hindsight, but Jack was visiting me every so often and monitoring me, so I was in good hands.

I was in such a state that Samantha had to link my arm to take me to the bathroom. A few days after I got home, Liam Creavin rang the house. He was ringing looking for my jersey from the match. Samantha answered the phone, and she should have told him the jersey was gone, it had been cut off me!

But she didn't. We had it, so she washed and ironed it, and handed it back. To be fair to Liam, he did ask how I was, but I think his main priority was getting the jersey back! There would be pure panic if a jersey went missing back then.

I was working for myself at the time, so the van was off the road for a while. It was a terrible belt, and I still get headaches to this day. I just had eyes on the ball, and... BANG! There was nothing malicious in it at all, it was just one of those things. I was out of football for a while after that. When I went back training, I have to admit that I was a bit anxious. If a high ball came in, I'd be a bit wary, looking around me and so on. Of course, you can't play football like that – you have to be one hundred percent committed.

WHAT REALLY GOT me back into things again was when St Michael's played Dunderry in the league in Carlanstown. I was centre-back or midfield, but I ended up back in the full-back line. I caught a ball and got an unmerciful belt in the back of my head. It was accidental, but I held onto the ball and cleared it out.

It was the best thing that ever happened me, because it gave me my confidence back. That's what I felt I needed. I suffer from headaches still and also suffer with a bit of vertigo, too. Whether it's to do with that bang or old age, I don't know. It took me about six or seven weeks to get back.

By the time the 1993 Leinster Championship came around, I was okay again. With a lot of new faces on the panel, I started to realise that I was now one of the more experienced players and I needed to step up another bit. I had seen a bit of the younger lads like Enda McManus and Graham Geraghty, so I knew what they were capable of. I had to take on the role that Mick Lyons and those lads had taken on with me when I joined the panel.

I had to put my arm around the new fellas, take them under my wing and help them along. Coyle would have done the same – we took on more responsibility. It was up to the so-called older lads to do that.

These lads who had come through minor and under-21 had the ability, so it was just a matter of helping them settle in. I think that's why the Meath team was so successful during that time – you had the old stock and then a few new faces. So when Mick, Gerry and Hayes went, myself and Coyle had to step up and some new young players came in. We needed them, and they needed us. But there was always a backbone there in terms of there being a core of experienced players. When you look at Meath teams in more recent times, there has often been so much change from year to year, that there's no backbone and everyone is coming in and having to do it for themselves. I always felt it was important to have a core of experienced players which you can add to with younger blood. Of course, that's not always possible.

We met Laois in the Leinster quarter-final, and it was probably the biggest influx of new faces in a long while. Enda was full-back, Geraghty was wing-back. I was centre-back. Cormac Murphy was on the other wing, Jody Devine was in, and McDermott was in. When someone new came onto the panel, Sean would introduce them around, but of course we'd have known them as some of those lads were on the 1990 minor team that won the All-Ireland.

Regardless of that, Sean would always introduce them to us. It was part of helping them feel welcome. I would find myself looking at these lads in training and sizing them up, wondering if they were going to be good enough to take over from the lads who had retired. At the same time, I knew that Sean wouldn't have them in there unless they were up to it.

Cormac Murphy was new, and he wasn't a man to take a backward step. You'd hear him before you'd see him! Cormac was one of these jolly fellas, but he took everything very seriously and he was very vocal. You'd think he'd been there for 10 years even though he was only in the door. He wouldn't have been shy about getting onto lads in training if he thought they weren't putting it in. That's how cocky Cormac was, that's how he played. He'd talk the hind legs off an ass. At first you'd nearly hate him, but that wouldn't last long. He was one of these lads that you could never fall out with.

When I got married, I was living in Beechmount in Navan, and he used to always call up to my house to chat about things. So he really looked up to me. Geraghty and Jimmy McGuinness used to call in, too, and we'd have great discussions. Cormac would be asking me what to do in certain situations, if his man got a ball here or there and so on. I would always tell him to stay on his feet as much as possible, not to dive in, that kind of thing.

Young fellas probably looked up at me at that time, given I'd been on the panel a while, and they'd pick my brain about different things. I was happy to do it. I would say that if I had gone up to O'Rourke's house or Lyons' house when I started, they'd have done the same for me, but I didn't have the confidence to do that. But these new boys did.

I would have classed myself as a father figure at that stage, and Samantha was great with them, too. She'd have tea for them, so there was always a good welcome in our house. At that time we had no kids, so these 'so-called kids' would call up and we'd have a great chat. You could spend an hour or two chatting and it would pass the evening, then you'd see them at training the following night, so we had a bond then which was great.

But I admired the lads for coming around and asking for advice. It showed that they cared, that they wanted to improve. I have to say though, I wouldn't have been one for the cocky approach. I would have been the opposite – come in quietly and work your way up. You need different characters though, that's what makes a dressing-room.

I HEARD A story once which reminded me a bit of Cormac. The great Dublin team of the 1970s were training and Kevin Moran had only just recently joined the panel. They were doing laps one night and Kevin was up the front, while some of the older lads were down the back.

So Kevin let a roar at a few of them to get up to the front. That's how cocky he was – and you see what he went on to achieve with Dublin and Manchester United. So maybe Cormac Murphy heard that story, too, because he came in and acted the very same way!

He was one fella I would have hated to mark. I hope he won't mind me saying that he wasn't the best footballer Meath has ever had but, my God, if you asked him to do a job and mark someone, he would follow that man to the toilet if he had to. He was such a tight marker, and he would do whatever he was told.

He didn't fear anyone either. He ended up marking Keith Barr in 1993, his first championship game against Dublin, and it wouldn't have bothered him for a second. He didn't care who he was marking, he just took them on. He was a hardy bit of stuff, very determined, and he wore his heart on his sleeve. That's why a lot of Meath supporters loved him.

He was also a perfect example of the knack Sean had for seeing something in a fella. When you look at the Meath teams for his time in charge, not all of the players were superstar senior club footballers. Sean was able to pick lads out from Junior or Intermediate football and see something in them, including myself. That team of 1987 up to '90 or '91, most of those lads played out around the middle of the field for their clubs. But Sean was able to put them in to certain positions and get something out of them.

Maybe having lads who arguably weren't the greatest natural footballers in the world worked to our advantage, because they were willing to work hard and do whatever it took to get onto the team and stay there, and Sean was able to get the most out of them. Even when there were lads who might have had a bit of an ego, Sean was always able to keep their feet on the ground. You were only as good as your last game with Sean.

It was a huge step for Sean after 1992 when a lot of that first team that he had built broke up. He had to put a new side together, but it was nothing new to him in one sense, because he had done it with us.

I found it a bit strange stepping into that father role, but I knew I had to step it up in terms of training and everything else, because these lads coming in were good footballers and they didn't give a shit about the likes of me. I would help them out and do whatever was needed to assist them in games, but in training I had to get my fitness back to where I wanted it to be, because these lads were after my place at the end of the day.

I'd say Coyler was thinking the same. Nobody was taking my place without a fight, and that's how it was when I came in, and how it always should be. They made everybody step up.

New faces might have come in but, by and large, training was the same from year to year. We had the Hill of Tara and we did all our stamina training there, then there was Bettystown where we'd be up in the sand dunes, and out in the water up to your belly-button running and it freezing cold – this was in the winter.

It was good for horses and Sean always said what was good for horses was good for us. We did Dalgan, we did Páirc Tailteann - up and down the stand and the terrace. I remember doing the Hill of Tara for three or four weeks, and you wouldn't see a ball. Well, actually, you would. Sean would arrive and take out the footballs, and we'd all be thinking... *Great! A bit of ball work tonight.*

Then Sean would put them back in the boot of the car. He'd just take them out to tease us I think, then we'd be off doing laps. That would have been our pre-season. We would do five or six weeks of the Hill of Tara three times a week. We'd be up there for the guts of two hours each night. I'd say the circuit we'd have done would be maybe four or five kilometres, and we'd do five or six laps of that. We'd do a bit of speed work on the hills – jog down and sprint up. We'd do long sprints, maybe 100 yards up hill.

Tough, tough stuff.

One morning, we were in Páirc Tailteann and there was snow on the ground. We'd been running up and down the stand. Next thing, Sean made us take off our boots and he ran us across Páirc Tailteann from one corner to another about 10 times in our bare feet in the snow. You'd think it was mad stuff, but it did us no harm. If people saw us doing it they would probably say, 'Seán Boylan is mad', but that's how Sean had us.

If he told us that sticking our head in the fire would make us a better player, we'd all do it. He had that grip on us. Now, there would have been a few lads asking… *What the hell is this about?* But we just got on and did it.

We had no choice. We'd train in hail, sleet or snow.

I WAS AT it a long time at that point.

I'd have been over 10 years with Meath at that stage, not including my little sabbatical in 1987! But I never found it hard to motivate myself to go training, even though it didn't change too much each year. It was just something that had to be done, so I put any thoughts of it being the same to one side.

I hear lads in teams I've coached complaining about training, that there isn't enough ball work or whatever, but if anyone can come up with a way of getting fit that doesn't involve running, I'm all ears. You have to run to get fit – it's that simple. I never got fed up with Sean's training. You knew what was going to happen, but maybe you were better off knowing.

The only thing I would have against Sean was when he'd tease us with the footballs. There was no need to do that! Even over at Bettystown some nights he'd get them out and we'd be delighted, then the little so-and-so would put them back in the car!

I always thought that knowing what you could expect was better than not knowing, and I think a lot of the lads would agree with that. We knew that during those five or six weeks, we were going to have the legs run off us. But it had to be done, and that was the only time to do it.

We might then have a challenge match to open a pitch, and our legs would be like jelly. That game against Kildare in Summerhill in 1989 when we didn't score – that was an example. The training had to be done then, because once you were into the championship, it was too late. Sean always had us fresh and always had us peaking at the right time. Some lads would have been thinking about the first round game when we were on those long runs - that would be their way of getting through it.

I never did that. I was just thinking about getting through that session! I would just have been focused on getting as fit as I could. Sean would have these tracks, and the first week you mightn't know where you were going, but as the weeks went on you'd know. The runs would get longer and longer. Some nights, Sean would take us one way on a short route, the next he'd take us on the long one.

So I certainly wouldn't have been thinking too far beyond my next step at that stage – the main thing was to get fit, and there was no better place than Tara to get you fit.

Once the championship started, it was mostly ball work and speed work. An odd night, Sean might bring us to Tara out of the blue, and we might just do a few laps and come home. There were nights in Dalgan where we'd do the speed work, then the following night we'd do nothing but stretching. We might stretch for an hour, then do a lap and that'd be it.

I think to this day that you can't do enough stretching, and I think Sean was ahead of his time in that regard, because I don't know how many teams would have spent an hour stretching at a training session. Even now I see soccer players doing stretches that I would have done with Sean 25 years ago, so I think that says it all about his methods. As the years went by, he'd take us to the swimming pool a bit and have us in the buoyancy suits. So he'd throw in the odd curveball to keep us guessing.

One thing which probably has changed over the years is the dietary side of things. There were no dieticians when I played. After training, we'd always go back to Bellinter House and we'd have a four-course meal. We'd have soup, a main, dessert, tea or coffee. And this could be at nine o'clock or later, and we'd go home with a bagful of steaks from Noel Keating. So there was no mention of diet, and I still think to this day that it was great. I'd go back to it again. I think eating the spuds and brown bread did me no harm, and

Sean would tell you the same. We were treated like kings and we were never told what to eat. It was eat whatever you want to eat, but it was all good wholesome stuff. Apart from dessert! That would be sherry trifle, or apple tart and ice-cream or black forest gateaux. Ina, who was the chef, and her staff looked after us so well, as did the nuns in Bellinter at that time.

A TRUE LEGEND in Meath football made himself known at this time.

John McDermott.

I remember John coming onto the panel in 1991, then he played in '92 against Laois and got a bad wallop and had to go off. I have to hold my hands up, I didn't see it in him at the time. At that stage he was playing football with Curraha – no disrespect to them, they've progressed on massively since then – but they were Junior at the time. I remember thinking… *Who's this long-legged fella?*

I couldn't see anything in him, and he'd probably murder me for saying that. How wrong I was. He turned out to be one of the best midfielders Meath ever had, and one of the best in the country when he was at his peak. Sean saw something in him, and it was probably 1993 or '94 when he really started to make his mark, so he'd been in there for a few years at that stage. It probably took him that length of time to get to that level, similar to me in a lot of ways.

John was very wiry when he came in first, just like I was, and it took those few years training at that level to build up his body. But other managers might not have seen what Sean saw in John and others. Maybe moving to Skryne and playing senior football helped John, but mainly you'd have to say he helped himself – he turned himself into the player he became. It was a bit like when Mick O'Dwyer brought the Bomber Liston into the Kerry panel and he was a few stone overweight and people wondered what Micko was at. The Bomber is a household name now, so some managers see things in players that not everyone would see. They work hard with them and make something out of them. Other managers might let these lads go after a month or two.

Given that Laois had beaten us in 1992, we were expecting a tough game against them in '93, especially as it was in O'Moore Park. It didn't turn out that way. We put in a really good performance that day and won comfortably. That set up a Leinster semi-final against Dublin. As I've said before, any Meath team I played on measured themselves against Dublin, so I was curious to see how we would fare with the new faces who had come in and how they would react to the occasion. We came up just short, but I needn't have worried about any of the lads.

It was another really tight game, and Dublin led by one going into added time. We got a free about 50 metres out, and Stafford played it short to Colm, and he wound up and kicked one of those trademark Colm O'Rourke points. It seemed to hang in the air for an age before dropping over.

Level again, and it looked like we were going to have another replay. The kick-out came, and Dublin got a chance, but Bob made a fantastic, full-length block on Charlie Redmond. We didn't get the luck on this occasion though, because the ball broke to Jack Sheedy. He just put the head down and drove it over the bar from about 45 metres.

Jack would probably tell you, he was erratic enough at times so that could have gone anywhere, a bit like Beggy in 1991. It sailed over, and that was it. The final whistle went shortly after. It was payback time for Dublin. They did to us in '93 what we did to them in '91.

CHAPTER **15**

AYRTON SENNA DIES FOLLOWING CRASH

"Ayrton Senna, perhaps the greatest racing driver of all time, was killed when he crashed at high speed while leading the San Marino Grand Prix at Imola yesterday. The 34-year-old Brazilian had dominated grand prix racing for the past decade, winning three world championships and 41 races. Senna's death follows an accident on Saturday that claimed the life of the 31 year-old Austrian driver, Roland Ratzenberger."

MEATH'S NEW MIX MAKES MAJOR IMPACT

Meath 2-11 Armagh 0-8

"Meath played great football in winning their seventh league title, showing that they have got together a very effective combination of old and young players with talent and experience spread evenly between them. But it was the older players – a relative term – who made the greatest impact. The 'old man' of the team, the 'general' to wit, Colm O'Rourke, was outstanding. The full-forward, Tommy Dowd, a youngster by comparison, destroyed the Armagh defence, while Martin O'Connell and Graham Geraghty were majestic in the winners' defence."

The Irish Times

THERE WAS A positional change for me in 1993. Having played most of my football, and certainly all my best football for Meath, in the half-back line, Sean came to me and said he wanted to try me at full-back. I wasn't going to say no.

I would have played anywhere. I wouldn't have been feared at full-back as much as Mick Lyons, but I slotted in fine. I called Mick up and asked him for a few pointers. He told me, 'Don't change your game... you're marking someone just the same as you are at wing-back.'

I still felt pressure when I switched, because if I made a mistake at wing-back, there was someone behind to cover. At full-back, I was more exposed if I did something wrong. Thankfully, I didn't make any big mistakes. I enjoyed it. When you've No.3 on your back, you think you're Mick Lyons!

I was never going to be another Mick, but maybe I felt a little bit braver or stuck my chest out the way Mick used to do, but he was different class compared to me. Maybe I was a bit nervous at first in case I'd make a mistake, but I must have done okay if I spent three years there. A lot of Meath supporters seem to think that we had no full-back between Mick retiring and Darren Fay coming along!

I can tell them now that we did. It was me!

We were in Division Two of the league that year, and we finished top along with Laois. We beat Down in the quarter-final, then we played Westmeath in the semi-final. Mattie Kerrigan was over them at the time, and Mattie knew everyone on that Meath team – where our weaknesses were, and where our strengths lay. Westmeath had a very good full-forward that time, Larry Giles and I remember Mattie shouting at him.

'Run him… RUN HIM!'

Maybe Mattie thought I was the weakness being in at full-back given it was a new position for me. Giles definitely got the better of me in the first-half, but I got to grips with him in the second. That was when Mattie came out and started roaring to pull me out of the square. I didn't answer Mattie back, because I had too much respect for him, but that got my dander up.

Thankfully, we held out and finished strongly, but it was a tough game which we only won by four points.

To be back in a national final was a huge deal for me and I was really looking forward to it. I was 30 at that stage. I knew I was coming towards the end. I might have maybe four years left, if I was lucky, and I treated that game like an All-Ireland final.

To be back on the big stage in a final was huge for all of us, but for me especially. Bob O'Malley was captain, so we had a few older lads and then a few new lads like Tom Hanley, Neville Dunne, Jim McGuinness and Trevor Giles. There was a big crowd there. The Cusack Stand had been knocked as the first part of the redevelopment of Croke Park, so all the crowd was on the

Hill, Canal and Hogan Stand. We knew Armagh were going to be a threat, because they had some great players.

I WAS ON Ger Houlahan, who was scoring goals to beat the band. The two semi-finals had been played on the same day in Croke Park, and he had a blinder against Laois. I saw a bit of him on television, and I imagined everyone asking, *'Who's going to be able to handle this Ger Houlahan fella?'*

I really built myself up to mark him in that final. He had scored a goal into the Hill in the semi-final, and I said to myself that that wouldn't happen against us.

After games in Croke Park at that time I used to meet some of my club mates and some of my family in McGrath's in Drumcondra, and then we'd go up to the Skylon Hotel. After the semi-final, I walked into McGrath's and there was a group of Armagh fans in the corner, and they all started shouting over.

'Houly's gonna get ya!

'Houly's gonna get ya!'

It was all good-natured and a bit of craic. I just laughed and thought to myself... *We'll see!*

I had a few pints, and headed off.

The final came around a couple of weeks later, and I could do nothing wrong. Any high balls that came in, I caught them. I was always out in front. I think Houlahan only had two shots.

He scored a point, and he hit the crossbar. Everything fell my way. We played really well that day, and Bernard Flynn getting two goals after being out for so long topped it all off. I was delighted for him, and thrilled that I had had a good game, because I felt under a lot of pressure to perform. Mick Lyons, who was a selector at the time, came over to me after the game.

'I thought you were finished two years ago,' he told me, 'but after today... you're only starting.'

It was great to hear that from him. We went up onto the Hogan Stand after the game, and it felt like winning the All-Ireland. Bob got the cup and said his few words. I thought this was going to be my last hurrah.

Time was running out for me. It was great, and in many ways, I got a bigger kick out of winning that league title than out of winning an All-Ireland, because it had been so long since I'd been up there.

I was so motivated for that game, not just because of the Houlahan stuff, but also because I was in a new position and I was getting on a bit, so I probably felt like I had to prove myself all over again. I trained really hard – both with Sean and on my own – which I felt I had to do once I got over the 30 mark. It really paid off for me.

I would say a lot of people in Meath were worried about whether I'd be able to handle him, but thankfully I was. Armagh had a really good team then, they were up-and-coming. Jarlath Burns was midfield, Kieran McGeeney was centre-back. They had Ger Reid and Diarmuid Marsden, so they were a good side. It was a great performance from us that day though. Flynn got his two goals, Geraghty was bombing forward from wing-back, O'Rourke played well, new lads like Tom Hanley and Neville Dunne had a good game. There was a great balance to that team.

When we won that league title, I really believed that team was good enough to win an All-Ireland. O'Rourke thought the same. I thought that 1994 team was going to kick on and we'd win more than just a league. I was very confident about the lads around me.

We got over Laois in Navan in the Leinster quarter-final. Páirc Tailteann was packed to the rafters that day because it was Laois again and that rivalry was massive for those few years. Pat Roe and Tommy Dowd had an almighty battle; I think Roe got the line in the end. It was a really exciting game, and I remember Flynn popped up with a few late points that got us through. We beat Wexford easily in the semi-final, so it was back to meet Dublin again in our first Leinster final since 1991.

THE BIG CONTROVERSY which many people will remember in the lead-up to that game was Donal Smyth leaving the panel. There were fierce rumours going around that Donal was going to be dropped off the panel. I don't know how that got out, but it filtered out somehow. Whether the selectors thought he wasn't up to it, I don't know.

I was into training in Dalgan Park one of the evenings in the lead-up to the final, and the selectors were there. Sean, Mick Lyons and Joe Cassells (who would have been Donal's clubmate). They were there before anybody, which would have been slightly unusual. I remember Donal going in to see them in front of me, and I thought to myself that it was a little odd.

Little did we know. We all togged out and went out onto the field, and passed no remarks. Next thing, we were all out on the field, and there was no sign of Donal. I think what happened was Donal left and went into training with the O'Mahonys – he told me that after. What happened between him and the selectors was none of my business.

It was hard though, a lot of lads were scratching their heads wondering what was going on. It wasn't a great morale-booster going into a big game.

Mickey McQuillan was back training the next night, and that was that. It wasn't ideal and the timing wasn't great, but the selectors obviously felt they had to make that call. Donal played on the Meath minors with me, and was a top goalkeeper who was winning championships with O'Mahonys left, right and centre. His kick-outs were very good, and there was one thing I'd say about Donal – he was never too shy about calling. He'd always be roaring at you and telling you where you should be. I think I turned around in one match and told him to shut the fuck up!

He was constantly at it, even if the ball was at the other end of the field, but it was great because he kept you on your toes. Mickey McQuillan wasn't quite as vocal, but Donal – you'd always hear him. That was the Garda in him coming out! It was unfortunate what happened, and I'd say Donal was very hurt about that. He had been there for so long, and had been understudy to Mickey for a long time, too. He hung in there when other lads might have walked.

IF YOU HAD to script what happened in that Leinster final after what had happened in the build-up, you would have had to put Mickey at the centre of it. That was how it turned out. What everyone remembers is that free-kick from Charlie Redmond under the Hogan Stand.

It was a wet day and I was on the left post, with Mickey in the middle.

I said to Mickey to come more towards where I was and I'd move out a bit, because I didn't think Redmond would have the distance to make it to the far post. I thought it would drop wide on the Nally Stand side of the goal. So I moved out about five or six yards, and the ball came in and it just went through Mickey's hands and dropped into the net.

Maybe if I'd stayed where I was, I might have caught it, or it might have gone through my hands, too. Who knows? It was just unfortunate.

Graham Geraghty got a great goal, and we got it back to a point, but that free knocked the stuffing out of us and we lost by one. Mickey's head was down at the end. I went back to him after the final whistle, what else could you do.

He was devastated.

It was a horrible way to lose. So, would people have said that the decision backfired on the selectors? Maybe, it was hard to know. It was a tough call for everyone involved and it just didn't quite work out, though Mickey had a good game other than that, and made a couple of excellent saves. Down the years, he had kept us in games, but unfortunately some of us – myself included – are remembered for negative incidents at certain times.

I'd say Mickey will be remembered for that, which is a shame, given all the great years he'd had with us. It was a difficult situation for him, but once he got the call to come back in, he was never going to say no. If we'd won the game, it was a masterstroke bringing him back. That's sport. These things happen.

I know when I came back in 1987 and played in that Leinster final, I felt the pressure, so I can imagine Mickey felt the same. He was gutted in the dressing-room after, and that turned out to be his last ever game for Meath. I would have known Mickey a long time, and I really felt for him. But as a fella said, no-one died.

What could you do? You could sit in the dressing-room all night, but it wasn't going to change the result.

The other thing about that game was that it was Trevor Giles' first time facing the Hill in a Leinster final, and he missed a couple of frees that day. It just shows you how tough a place it can be, especially when you look at the player Trevor went on to become.

There's no better place to learn though, because I used to take the 45s for Meath way back, and you'd be hitting them into Hill 16 and they'd be constantly booing. It is off-putting, no doubt about that. It was a game we could have won, and it was disappointing after winning the league. But we had our chances and didn't take them, so it certainly wasn't all down to Mickey.

Flynn caught a ball in the first-half and was just about to turn when John O'Leary nearly took the head off him. If we got a goal from that, it might have been different. But that's how it was with us and Dublin, there was always just the hop of a ball between us. They got the luck that day and we didn't. On other days, we got the luck.

DUBLIN BEAT LEITRIM handy enough in the semi-final.

I was invited over to New York for some function. A cousin of mine had a bar over there, a fella called Philip Sheridan. So I was in that bar at half ten in the morning, and Dublin hammered them. Séamus Quinn from Leitrim got an All Star at full-back that year – thanks to Colm O'Rourke – when I should have got it!

I was nominated, but on TV Colm praised Quinn from a height, and I remember looking and listening to this. Maybe I was getting ahead of myself thinking I was going to get an All Star. But then I reckon Colm spoiled my chances because he talked Séamus Quinn up so much! I told Colm that several times, but he'd just laugh at me, so he won't mind me telling him again. Dublin lost that year's All-Ireland to Down. We had come so close to beating them, and I think we would have gotten over Leitrim. It would have been great to get a chance for revenge against Down, but it wasn't to be.

What was odd about the Meath-Dublin games back then was that, even though every game aside from 1995 was close, the wins seemed to come in blocks. We beat them in 1986, '87, '88, then in 1990 and '91. Dublin won in 1993, '94 and '95. You might have expected it to be more tit-for-tat. I still maintain that if we had Mick Lyons in 1989, we'd have won six Leinsters in-a-row.

By the time of the 1995 championship, we had a new goalkeeper in the shape of Conor Martin, but the rest of the team was similar to the year before, with the exception of Bernard Flynn who had retired and was a big loss. We had Offaly in the first round in Navan, and the story again was about a high-profile omission from the starting line-up – Colm O'Rourke was dropped for probably the first time in his Meath career.

The two most memorable things about that game was there was a massive hailstorm early on, and Colm came on in the second-half and got a goal. It was a comfortable win in the end.

We had Wicklow in the semi-final in Portlaoise and were a bit wary of them after what had happened in 1991, when they nearly caught us. Kevin O'Brien was still there, and we didn't have the same team as we had then, so we were on our guard. We got a couple of early goals and the game was over after five minutes.

I was full-back that day and I don't think the ball came near me in the first-half. We were that dominant in the forwards and midfield. We won by 14 points in the end. Colm was back in the starting 15 and got another goal, so all was right with the world as we headed into yet another Leinster final. Everything was, as usual, pointing to a tight game between ourselves and Dublin, but it turned out to be one of the worst days any of us had seen in a Meath jersey.

We got the ideal start, with Jody Devine kicking a point right from the throw-in, but we weren't playing particularly well as the half went on. It was tit-for-tat just like it always was in those games. I was marking Jason Sherlock for a while, then he moved onto Coyler. We went in four down at half-time, but we started the second-half really well. Evan Kelly palmed in a goal, and Graham kicked a point a few minutes later.

That put us a point up 15 minutes into the second-half. I thought we were coping well enough with Dublin's forwards at that time and it looked like we were on top. Then the wheels game off.

Dublin went back in front, then Sherlock got a ball and went for a point, but skied it. It dropped down in front of the goal and Paul Clarke fisted it into the net. To this day, I don't know what happened us at the end of that game, but Dublin tagged on a heap of scores. There were 10 points in it at the end. Maybe our heads went down for the first time, there were a lot of young lads on that team.

Dublin at that time had a bit more experience than we did. Maybe that was part of it, but we just fell apart in the last quarter of that game. That Dublin team had a bit of a harder edge to them, and I would say that came from Pat O'Neill. Pat was a tough, hard player when he played. He brought a little bit more steel to Dublin when they were playing us. They had a bit of steel anyway, but they played more on the edge when O'Neill came in - they seemed a bit braver and a bit more fired-up.

JOE AND MICK were selectors for us that year and Mick, even though it was great that he was involved when we won the league, said it was the worst thing he ever did – coming in as a selector when lads he had soldiered with were still playing. Mick was there in 1994 when Donal got dropped, and I know he found it very hard. He thought he would have made enemies by staying around any longer.

I think he would say now that he should have waited until all the lads were gone before coming in. I don't know if Joe would have thought the same, but Mick definitely thought he made a mistake coming in. From my perspective, it didn't bother me that Mick was there. It was a bit strange to have lads who you played with in as part of the backroom team, and I'm sure it was strange for them, too. But I didn't pass any remarks, and Sean was still the manager, so ultimately it was him who was making the calls.

After that game, there was a lot of talk of clearouts.

Talk of people retiring, talk of Sean's time being at an end. Personally, I never thought about giving it up. We came into the dressing-room after the game and there was barely a word said. To be beaten by 10 points was humiliating. No other word for it. I had great hopes for that 1994 team winning something, and we nearly won the Leinster final that year. In 1995, I thought the same again. We'd pushed Dublin so close in 1994 that we should surely drive on. To lose by 10 points was just disastrous.

It was like someone had died in the dressing-room, there was complete silence. Nobody from Dublin really rubbed it in. Paul Clarke said a few things, and myself and Coyler gave him a bit of a push. Paul would be a nice fella off the pitch, but he was a bit arrogant on it – and there's no harm in that. It was easy saying things when you're six or seven points up! But there was nothing in it really, there would have been good respect there between the sides.

Nobody at that time was mentioning Sean Boylan going, because it wouldn't have been the thing to do. But as the weeks and days passed, you started hearing people saying, 'Oh, Boylan's finished... he should pack it in'. That kind of stuff. I took a day off work on the Monday which I would never usually have done. We met in Bob O'Malley's pub. I think pretty much everyone was there, all the players. We were chatting and talking about whether this was the end of the road.

'Will Sean go?'

'What do you think?'

I was sitting next to Colm Coyle at one stage and I said to him, 'I'm not going anywhere. I'm going to give it another go and I'll keep going for as long as I can. I don't want to quit.'

Coyler said the same. I didn't think it was the end by any means for that team. I would never have thought that. We had lost a few, but we had good lads coming in. Giles was going to get better, Geraghty was going to get better, McManus was going to get better.

I was captain that year, too. But I was one of those fellas who, hammering or no hammering, just wanted to play football. So that's why I didn't retire. The supporters on the field after that game, they were still patting us on the back, they appreciated us. I'd say a lot of them thought that this was the end of an era. A bit like in 1992 when we lost and were clapped off the field. A few left after 1992, and a few more left in '95.

I'd say the manner of the defeat might have fed into that. If it was a point or two, maybe you'd say... *I'll go again.* But 10 points? O'Rourke went, Bob went, Stafford went, and PJ went (even though he came back in 1997).

It was easy to name the older lads who stayed – myself and Colm Coyle. There's never really a good time to go, as I found out soon after. Sean probably felt the same. I mean, do you go out after running Dublin close? Do you go out after beating Dublin? You certainly can't go after being beaten by 10 points. So, there were all these questions to consider. If I was Sean Boylan at the time, having been beaten by Dublin by 10 points, there was no way I would have stepped away.

I would have kept going and got another crack at them, and see where that would lead.

I don't think anyone getting a beating like that was going to throw the towel in, and Sean certainly didn't. But Bob finishing up that year was a pity, because I thought he had a couple more years left in him, just like I did. He took it very seriously and I would say he would have been disappointed to have been taken off in that Leinster final.

AFTER 1995 I was a bit nervous that the call might not come to go back for the following year, even though I didn't think I had a bad year. I felt really good at that time, and I always thought I'd be asked back.

When the call did come though, I'd always be relieved to get it. I really couldn't have foreseen what happened in 1996. At the time I probably thought that was it. I'd walked off the pitch a few months earlier having been beaten by 10 points by our biggest rivals.

CHAPTER 16

SATURDAY, JULY 27, 1996

THE PRIDE OF IRELAND

"Swimming legend, Michelle Smith added an incredible fourth Olympic medal to her Atlanta tally earlier today. The 26 year-old superstar scooped bronze in the last, and toughest, race of an unforgettable Olympic week. Her bid for a fourth gold, and a place in the Olympic record books, was denied by Australian Susan O'Neill, the world 200m butterfly champion."

COULD BE LAST THROW OF DICE FOR BOYLAN

"Sean Boylan is one of the country's longest-serving managers, a last chance saloon appointment when nobody else wanted to sit on the Royal throne. Last year, he stood under the Hogan Stand in the tight corridor between the dressing-rooms, and good-naturedly rebuffed questions from equally good-natured journalists about his future with the team. Boylan can't go on forever, can he? The radical overhaul of the side would seem to indicate that he is getting itchy feet. Although the Meath team is in a state of evolution, it could be one last throw for Boylan."

The Irish Independent

THE LEAGUE OF 1995-96 went fairly well for us.

We beat Offaly, Laois, Clare, Kerry and Tyrone. The talk in the papers was that Sean's rebuilding project was coming along nicely. He was trying lads out in different positions. John McDermott played a few games at centre-back, and Jody played at wing-back once or twice. I don't think he planned to play either man there long-term, but I think Sean liked to give fellas a taste of a different position so they could understand a bit more about what was involved in playing in defence, for example.

We got to a league quarter-final, but lost to Mayo which was a bit disappointing. Overall though, it was a good league because Sean had been able to bring in a lot of new faces, and they had all done fairly well. I had been captain in 1995 and Sean had asked me would I stay on in that role in '96. I had a think about it, but I had been captain in '92 and '95. Beaten by Laois in Navan the first year and humiliated by Dublin the second! So I told Sean that he better find someone else, I was a bad omen. He went with Tommy Dowd, which didn't work out too badly.

We went into the Leinster championship, and we had Carlow in the first round. There was a real fear in the county that we were going to get done. Even the crowd that day was poor – a lot of Meath supporters didn't go to that match. Éire Óg were after getting to the All-Ireland club final earlier that year, and Carlow had a good few of those lads.

Some Meath people thought we might be in trouble, but the players certainly didn't feel that way. We were going up to Croke Park, and we were going to give it a shot. Meath – most of the time – played well up there. We absolutely hammered them. There were lads shooting from everywhere near the end.

Mark O'Reilly even came up and got a point. I think I had a shot, too!

In the week leading up to that game, I pulled something in the back of my knee, and I thought I was going to be out. But I got a big knee bandage and Sean put me through a fitness test. Maybe he feared Carlow, because he wanted to make sure I was fit. Maybe he was worried. I came through the fitness test and I played with the big blue knee bandage on me. I felt great. We won by 24 points to six. In the space of one game, not only did the team believe in ourselves, but the supporters started to believe aswell.

I moved into the corner that year. I'm not sure why – maybe Seán didn't think I was comfortable enough at full-back. It worked out okay for me though. I was in the left corner, and I was so familiar with left half-back that I was arguably more comfortable in the left corner than at full-back. Darren Fay came in at full-back and Mark O'Reilly was in the other corner, so it was a whole new full-back line really.

Darren and Mark were young, so I had that bit of experience to sweep in around the two of them and they were able to sweep in around me, too. Maybe Sean thought my experience would bring something to the full-back line with the two lads coming in. They both settled in well and Darren went on to become one of the best full-backs Meath ever had. So it worked in their favour, and going into the corner worked in mine.

Paddy Reynolds was also new in that year. Jimmy McGuinness had gone to midfield, and Barry Callaghan came into the forwards. But, arguably, the biggest changes that year were positional, with Brendan Reilly and Graham Geraghty moving into the attack. Brendan had always played wing-back or corner-back for Meath. Graham, like me, played all over.

Now, Graham was a lot better than I was as a forward, but he was brilliant as a half-back, he was brilliant at midfield with his club, and he was brilliant for us at wing-forward. Later on, of course, he'd also make his mark at full-forward. He was one of those lads who could play anywhere. But Sean had that knack of putting lads here or there, out of the blue. Jimmy and John Mc in midfield were a great partnership.

Brendan, as far as I remember, would have played full-forward for his club a good bit. He was another one of those lads who could play anywhere. Though he hadn't played there for Meath before, it wasn't completely new to him. He had two great feet and was well able to score from any angle. As well as that, he was as hard as nails and really brave.

Some supporters might have given him a hard time, but he was very young when he came into the panel in 1988. Then he got his shoulder busted and had a few operations, so he was a great man to come back from that. Sean moved lads around a bit if he thought they had the qualities to do a job in a certain position. He would have been very flexible and open-minded about things like that.

AFTER WE GOT over Carlow, we had our old foes Laois in the Leinster 'semi'. I always feared Laois, they always gave us a tough time of it. Whether we played them in Croke Park or Navan or Portlaoise, we always found it hard to get past them. Nine times out of 10 we would get through, but it was always a bit of a battle. That game in 1996, though, was one of the easiest games we had against them for some reason. We beat them handy enough, which I didn't think was going to be the case. Brendan got a goal early enough and we never looked back after that.

So we were back into a Leinster final, but this time it was a bit different.

This time, we had that 10-point hammering to think about. Even though we had some new faces in the team, there were a lot of lads still there in 1996 who had played in '95. It wasn't a nice feeling coming off the field having lost to your biggest rivals by 10 points. So to get another crack at them so soon was massive. I was really wound up and determined that we weren't going to get beaten like that again. We didn't really need much motivation playing Dublin at any time, but that particular year, we had a lot of damage to repair. It really got us going.

The younger lads went out and settled into it really well. They expressed themselves. I was probably more nervous than anyone. I found that happened me the older I got, because every big game could be my last. It was a really wet, slippy day, and I was hanging out of Dessie Farrell all day long. He was complaining left, right and centre! He was out in front of me a fair bit, but no ball ever stuck with him. I got a hand in or I gave him a bit of a pull. But he was always complaining to the referee, and I was always in his ear.

'Jesus Dessie, would you stop complaining. Cop onto yourself!'

I fouled him a good bit, but it was one of those days when everyone were slipping and sliding, and it didn't look as obvious as it might on a dry day. So I'll hold my hands up and say maybe I got away with murder, but I held him to a point and he was one of their danger men.

Colm Coyle was playing out the field, and he was doing fairly well. Paddy Reynolds was on Ciarán Whelan, who was making his debut for Dublin that day. Paddy was left half-back, so he was in front of me. Paddy was a divil for going up the field. He'd never cover me, and the last thing I wanted at my age playing corner-back was a half-back who was gone and would leave 50 or 60 yards in front of me. I was nearly going to get a rope and tie it around him to pull him back! Every time I looked up the field, he was gone! I don't know how many times I got onto him about it, even at half-time.

'Don't go any further than midfield!'

But I don't think he paid too much attention! For a lot of games, the ball was only thrown in and he would be gone like a greyhound out of a trap! So there were plenty of times that year where I was really sweating that the ball was going to come in quicker than it did. I wouldn't mind if Paddy was a half-back that could score, but that wasn't really his game. In fairness to him, Paddy did well on Whelan that day even though he was much smaller. Whelan got a couple of points, but Paddy stuck at it.

He was a great man to get onto breaking ball. Fay did well on Sherlock, and O'Reilly was able to handle Redmond. All over the field, the young lads were more than holding their own, and the more experienced guys were doing their bit. Enda McManus was solid at centre-back, so nothing really came up the middle.

Dublin brought the best out of us that day, more so than the likes of Carlow and Laois. In those conditions, it wasn't a classic game but we really knuckled down. It was a bit like 1986 all over again. Dublin were champions, it was a horrible day and scores were hard to come by.

We were two down with 10 minutes to go, and we got the last four points. Tommy Dowd got one of them – and Tommy was after getting busted in a clash with Keith Barr earlier. He went off, got a few stitches, and came back on.

There wasn't a bother on him. That's just the way he was. They were All-Ireland champions, and they were fairly sick after that.

I was a little bit nervous before the game, maybe because I'd have been thinking about doing two or three things rather than just doing my own job. I was probably worrying too much about dropping back a bit to cover the lads. We hadn't been tested that year at all. Carlow was easy, Laois was relatively easy. Then all of a sudden, we're playing Dublin. So it was a bit of a worry going out to see how lads would react playing against the All-Ireland champions, but everyone performed well.

During the game, whenever I got a chance, I'd have a quick word with them or give them a bit of advice, and maybe that helped a bit. I was always telling Fay to play in front of his man, but Darren was very good under a high ball, and he was very quick, so he could play it whatever way he wanted. I always played slightly behind. I never liked a fella turning me, because if he did turn me, I was gone.

Darren had the pace that if he was turned, he was able to get back. I found I got a little bit more vocal the older I got. When Mick was gone, I felt like I needed to take on that responsibility, and especially once I moved back into the full-back line, I could see everything. When I was in the half-back line, I could only see bits and pieces. So I became a lot more vocal when I moved back.

Darren would have been quiet enough, he wouldn't have done a whole lot of shouting, but I'm sure as he got older he would have done more of it, just like I did. Likewise with Mark O'Reilly – you'd never hear him shouting. They took everything on board, but I was probably doing enough shouting for the whole full-back line! Further out, Coyler was very vocal, and Enda McManus was well-enough experienced at that stage, too. Up front, there weren't too many inexperienced lads. Barry Callaghan was new, but he'd have had Brendan Reilly in his ear, and Tommy too. There was plenty of experience for the young lads to lean on in games.

THAT WAS OUR first Leinster title since 1991, which was a lifetime for Meath back then. Winning the league in 1994 had been huge for me, so to get up the steps of the Hogan Stand after the Leinster final in '96 was just fantastic. I could just sense that I was coming to the end though.

Against Dessie Farrell that day, I knew I was slowing down a bit, even though I was still doing extra training on my own. A few times, if the ball had come in that little bit quicker, I'd have been got at. It was bound to come to an end fairly quickly, and the years were starting to catch up on me. I probably thought more of that Leinster title that I did of any of the others – even the first one in 1986. It was probably the best Leinster final that I ever won. The age I was, being in a new position, and the fact that it was fairly unexpected. I'd always have been fairly confident going onto the field, and I'd never tell anyone we've no chance but, in other years, we'd nearly have expected to win a Leinster. That year, I don't think anyone would have said they were too confident. That made it all the more special.

While the conditions were similar to 1986, the attitude was much different in the aftermath of that '96 final. We celebrated winning the Leinster, but that was that. We had beaten the All-Ireland champions, and we were one game away from an All-Ireland final.

Up next was Tyrone. The first team for 20 years to retain the Ulster title. Narrowly, and controversially, beaten in the 1995 All-Ireland final.

Defeat would also be their lot in 1996 and, once again, there would be no shortage of controversy.

CHAPTER 17

MONDAY, AUGUST 19, 1996

AFTER ALL, IT'S A WONDERGOAL

"In the ideal world, Alex Ferguson would no doubt prefer David Beckham's England career to stay on hold for a while little longer. The stunning goal from 55 yards, 23 seconds into stoppage time in Manchester United's comprehensive 3-0 win at Wimbledon makes the case for Beckham's inclusion in the World Cup squad to play Moldova on September 1 almost irresistible."

MEATH CRUSH TYRONE TO BOOK FINAL PLACE

Meath 2-15 Tyrone 0-12

"It was not so much the victory but the manner of its execution which had so many gasping in admiration at Meath's crushing defeat of Tyrone in a wonderfully entertaining Bank of Ireland All-Ireland football championship semi-final at Croke Park yesterday. Tyrone fans travelled in vast numbers to swell the attendance to some 59,270, but a relentless series of points from a rampant Meath during the second-half left them with little option but to sit back and admire the skill and scoring power of the Royal County. Tyrone were outclassed at midfield, while those old wily defenders, Martin O'Connell and Colm Coyle, proved the wisdom of Sean Boylan in giving them one more chance."

Irish Independent

GOING INTO THAT 1996 All-Ireland semi-final, the feeling in the media was that this Meath team was a bit too young and a bit too green to beat Tyrone. They had just won back-to-back 'Ulsters', and had been beaten in the All-Ireland the year before. So a lot of people felt that it was almost written that they would come back and go one step further in '96. Naturally, we had other ideas.

Despite the fact that we hadn't met in the championship, we had come up against Tyrone a few times around then. We beat them in the league at the back end of '95 but, of more significance in many ways, were two challenge matches we played against them earlier in the season in 1996. We met once up in Irvinestown, and once in Navan.

Any player will tell you that, while you give challenges your best, you don't give them nearly the same level of commitment that you would give to a championship game. But in those matches, the Tyrone lads were going at it like it was championship. They were hitting us hard and getting the better of us all over the field, especially in that game in Navan. I think it was eight points to no score after about 20 minutes. They were running riot – we couldn't curtail them at all.

Sean got us in at half-time and he read the riot act, and we tore into them when we went back out. We won the second-half well, although Tyrone won the game. I think that did us the world of good. That game was early in the year and we still had a championship campaign to play, but we knew what Tyrone were about. We'd seen them on television before, but after playing against them, we knew what we were going to get if we met them later in the summer.

The semi-final started the very same way that the challenge matches had. Tyrone got a really quick start and went three points to no score up, and then four-one up. Peter Canavan got the fourth point for Tyrone and I clearly remember running back out after that score. The Tyrone fans were going mad – they outnumbered Meath fans by three-to-one, I'd say.

WHEN TYRONE RAN out onto the field that day, it was the noisiest Croke Park I've ever experienced in my life. I thought that stand was going to fall down, because the din was just incredible. With an atmosphere like that, it can either build you up or it can knock you for six.

Of course, for me, that game is remembered for a couple of clashes with Tyrone players. At least it certainly is in Tyrone, where they called me every name under the sun! We were really fired up, because there were things done in the game in Navan a few months earlier which stayed in my mind. Name-calling and different things like that… and we didn't do anything about it.

Now, I don't mean for one second that we were going into Croke Park to take the heads off lads, but we were really up for it.

We had also been told that they had gone up to Dublin the week before that game to record a song for the All-Ireland final. Whether that was true or not, I don't know, but we believed it! The first incident was between myself and Ciarán McBride. He went down on a ball under the Cusack Stand, and I kind of fell over him, and my knee clipped him on the head.

He went off the field with blood running out of him. When he came back on, you'd think he'd come back from a battlefield. He had a big bandage wrapped around his head for what was only a little nick.

About five or 10 minutes later, a ball came down the line in front of the Cusack Stand, and myself and Brian Dooher went for it. Looking back on it, it was a ball I should nearly have let Dooher get. Instead, I went over the top of him and he spun me.

He was a yard or so in front.

I knocked the ball out of his hand and, as I did, he fell over in front of me. The ball was hopping and, as I was going over him to try to win it back, I caught him on the head with my boot. I certainly didn't stamp on him. A stamp is looking down on a fella and putting real force into it.

I clipped him with my stud.

There certainly was no stamping motion involved, and I would defy anyone to say otherwise. I was in two minds that day whether to wear moulded or studs, and in the end I wore studs. If I'd have worn moulded, I probably wouldn't have cut him at all. It was definitely accidental.

I know some people said – and will still say – it wasn't, but it's over 20 years ago now and I still say it was an accident. I clipped him, but my eyes were on the ball. Like McBride, Dooher went off with blood everywhere.

Like McBride, Dooher came back out with a big bandage.

Only for the bandages, people wouldn't have noticed anything at all. It certainly wasn't my form to intentionally injure someone, it was just one of those things unfortunately. Play went on, and there was nothing said or done by the referee after either incident.

IF THERE'S EVER a game I look back on, or if there was a game to show young lads, that semi-final would be it. I think it was the best game we ever played in Croke Park, even better than any of the games in 1987 and '88.

Of any of the teams I was involved with, I think the '96 semi-final was the best. It was unreal. It was level at half-time (1-6 to 0-9), but we ended up scoring 2-15. We scored some great points and we just dominated all over the place – from Conor Martin out. Our backs were excellent, and Geraghty had the freedom of the park, scoring 1-4. They just couldn't live with him.

McDermott and McGuinness dominated around the middle... you couldn't pick out any one player, everyone from 1 to 15 was excellent. It was just one of those days where 15 lads played well – it rarely happens. It was brilliant to see it.

Great scores, great tackling, great blocking – we did all that. We beat them very comfortably in the end.

In any sport, it's always hard to explain why you perform so well on certain days and not so well on others, but on that occasion I really think the challenge matches were a big motivation. We started very slowly but we gradually got into it. Geraghty got the first goal – which put us in front for the first time – and we started tagging on a few points.

Sean gave us a good talking to at half-time, and we came flying out of the blocks in the second-half. Tyrone just couldn't cope with the pace and the physicality. I remember watching the game back, and a Tyrone selector said to RTÉ at half-time that we were much more physical, and we noticed that. When we got on top of Tyrone, we could see that they weren't going as hard for the ball as they were in the first 10 minutes.

Then Canavan was injured, which was a big blow for them. He stayed on the whole game, but he was limping. They just couldn't cope with it, and that was the bottom line. When you see what they've done since, they've toughened up, so maybe that game helped them in the long run. That particular day, everything went well for us. I won't say it went according to plan, because I don't think any of us expected it. I couldn't believe the performance we put in. It was just a pity the way it went for me. When the final whistle went, it was a fantastic feeling, but when the shit hit the fan a few days later it was a worrying time for me, which was unfair I thought.

When the game was over, I was enjoying the victory and didn't give a moment's thought to the incidents with McBride and Dooher. Little did

I know how bad it was going to get. That evening, *The Sunday Game* was inundated with calls, and letters started flooding into the newspapers. There was a big discussion about it on *Liveline* on the Monday.

Liveline! I couldn't believe it.

I got a call from a producer on the show asking would I go on and talk about it. I was out working in the van so I was busy. I hadn't the time to talk, and I had no intention of talking and fuelling the whole thing. So I was driving around and Colm O'Rourke was on, and Ciarán McBride was on, too, I think. I was hearing bits and pieces of this because I was in and out of the van, so I didn't hear it all.

Colm, of course, was standing up for me, McBride reckoned it was the toughest game he ever played in. I didn't think it was that tough. Those two incidents probably looked bad, but they weren't really. I stamped on nobody, that wasn't my form. John McDermott also got a bit of criticism over a tackle on Peter Canavan which injured him, but Tyrone weren't angels, we weren't angels, that's just the way it was.

I thought that would be the end of it and the whole thing would blow over after the Monday, but things got much worse.

With all the calls and letters, the GAA came under pressure to review the incidents, and there was talk that I was going to miss the All-Ireland final. I came home to Samantha one evening and said to her, 'I could be in a bit of bother here… I mightn't get to play in the final'.

Everyone was panicking, because nobody knew what was going to happen. I went over to my mother and father, and they were in bits over it, and this went on for the best part of two weeks. The game was played on August 18, and the GAC decision wasn't made public until 10 days later.

So, in the meantime, I was left wondering was I going to be suspended?

Was I going to be allowed to play? It was a horrible time. At my age, I knew it was probably going to be my last All-Ireland, so to miss out on it for something like that would have been devastating.

What I really remember at that time was Sean. He was just brilliant during those 10 days or so. We just carried on as if nothing had happened. It was hard because I'd be thinking about it, but I just put the head down and tried to get on with it as best I could. But still, when I was driving home in the car by myself, or driving around in the van during the day, I'd have been thinking the worst. Thinking that I might not be able to play.

Thinking that they might suspend me. Then I heard that Jack Boothman was on the committee, and he really loved Meath. So when I heard Jack was in there I thought… *I might be okay.*

I never got onto Jack, and Jack never go onto me.

One of the papers had a frame-by-frame set of pictures, which showed where I took off from, where Dooher's head was, where my eyes were… I can still see it. So I think the GAC's decision was based around the fact that I had my eyes on the ball.

I got it into my head that it was going to be okay, and that's what got me through. I finally got a phone call saying that I had been cleared to play. But it took the guts of two weeks, and it felt like a lot longer than that. I felt sorry for my mother and father during the whole thing, because they were more worried than I was. I was telling them all along that nothing was going to happen.

I MET DOOHER once since then, and that was at a function in Oldcastle in 1996. We were All-Ireland champions at the time, and all of us were down at this event. Dooher was about 20 yards away, and he had a bit of a cut on his cheek.

Coyle being Coyle, he said to me, 'I thought you walked on that fella's head? Are you not going to go over to say something to him?'

I was looking over at him and he was looking over at me, so I said… *Feck this, I'll make the first move. I'll go over to him.* I shook hands with him and I said, 'I thought I got you on the head, not on the cheek!'

'Oh, I cut myself shaving!' he replied.

We had a laugh and a joke about it, which I was glad about. You never want to fall out with lads, whether you played with them or against them.

In the winter of 1996, we played Tyrone in Omagh in the league. I got dog's abuse from their supporters. Sean had asked me beforehand if I'd prefer to be left at home, but I said no way. I didn't want people thinking I was afraid to go up.

I was called every name under the sun. At that time in Omagh, the dressing-rooms were a bit away from the pitch. We had to tog out, then run out through the crowd and down a tunnel onto the field. Tyrone gave us a guard of honour as we came out at the start of the game. We were well beaten in the end, but coming off at half-time I was met with all sorts of abuse as I made my way through the crowd back to the dressing-room.

In fairness to Dooher and Adrian Cush, they came in either side of me coming off the field. I'd have to applaud them for that. They told me to pay no attention to anything that was being said. On the way back out I got the same treatment from the Tyrone fans, and every time I got near the ball there'd be a big cheer or a big boo or something.

There was one ball I went for, and I knew that if I went down on it that I'd be absolutely killed, so I just pulled on it and it hit the barbed wire on the fence. It might have looked like I chickened out, but if I had gone down on the ball I'd have been buried!

I have to say that there was nothing from any of the Tyrone players – no hitting and no verbals. The verbals came from the crowd only, but that happens. If the roles had been reversed, the Meath fans would no doubt have given the same abuse to a Tyrone player. There's always a few.

It was the first time it had ever happened to me, so it was intimidating and was definitely the worst thing I had ever experienced. I had my brother and a few lads from the club with me, because I sensed that something was going to happen. I remember ringing him before the game.

'Make sure you're all together,' I told him, '... and when I'm coming on and off the field, don't be too far away!'

So, they had to be there four times and, in fairness to them, they were.

But it was decent of the Tyrone lads to look out for me. It would be nice to meet those lads again, the Mayo and Tyrone lads. We'd probably get on great, just like we did with the Cork boys when we got to know them. If we ever needed anything from the Cork lads, they'd come up, and vice-versa. But we didn't play Mayo or Tyrone as much as we did Cork, so that connection isn't as strong.

As much as it was a tough afternoon in Tyrone, it was the right thing to do to go up. I was man enough to do it and if I hadn't, I'd have been called a coward, which would have been far worse than what I was called at the game.

The other thing about that was that in the south, you'd always have a Garda presence at games, but in the North, the RUC – as it was at the time - didn't come near GAA grounds. They'd do the traffic outside and so on, but they'd stay out on the road. That might have changed now, but that time they didn't come in.

Mick Higgins, who was married to an aunt of mine, told me that. He used to train Cavan and had a bit of hassle with Tyrone himself years earlier. He told me to be careful when I'm up there because there'd only be stewards in the ground. In the end, it turned out fine. After the game, a few of the lads went into the bar in the clubhouse for a few drinks, but I just got back on the bus and waited.

I didn't want to be in a situation where there were players and fans mixing, and drink involved. It wasn't worth pushing my luck and taking a chance, even though I could have done with a drink at that stage!

I GOT A bit of 'fan mail' around that time, too – a few letters from disgruntled supporters. They were sent to the club. The envelopes would just have 'Martin O'Connell, St Michael's GFC, County Meath' written on them. Of course, no name was ever put to any of the letters. I got a handful, all posted from the north, all handwritten. It was after the 1996 All-Ireland when they started coming.

Telling me I was a thug and I didn't deserve an All-Ireland medal. They wouldn't even have been a full page. It didn't bother me for a second, because whoever sent them wasn't even brave enough to put their name to it.

Sean got a few, too, telling him that he sent us out to do it – to take lads out. No more than getting abuse at a game, it's usually a small minority, and when someone doesn't even have the guts to put their name to what they've written, that tells you all you need to know, doesn't it?

CHAPTER **18**

FRANKIE'S DREAM A NIGHTMARE FOR BOOKIES

"Punters on both sides of the Irish Sea were yesterday celebrating Frankie Dettori's record-setting seven winners at Ascot on Saturday. Ladbrokes, the world's largest booking chain, last night reported having their 'worst day' since moving into Ireland 10 years ago. It is believed that the firm was hit for £130,000 by a Dublin punter who laid out a total of £20. In Cork meanwhile, they have losses of at least £110,000 as a result of a £15 bet."

DOGGED MEATH CRUSH BRAVE MAYO'S DREAMS
Meath 2-9 Mayo 1-11

"Mayo won sympathy and copious plaudits but not the pot of silver, as dogged determination led Meath to All-Ireland football glory yesterday. Sean Boylan's never-say-die outfit scored a late point in a final tossed about by ferocious winds and played with 14 men apiece for 63 of the 70 minutes. Referee Pat McEnaney sent Liam McHale and Colm Coyle to the line after a violent outburst involving 20 players in the first ten minutes."

The Irish Examiner

I FELT REALLY good in the build-up to that 1996 All-Ireland final. The worry of the possible suspension arising from the semi-final was behind me, and I could focus fully on a crack at winning a third Celtic Cross. I was injury-free, looking after myself, and doing an extra bit of training.

The build-up was great, but then, the build-up to any All-Ireland final is great. There's always a great buzz in the county and I was walking around feeling 10-feet tall, although Sean would always keep our feet firmly on the ground. By that time I was used to it, because I'd played in a few of them and knew what was going to happen. All the usual boxes were ticked good and early. The press night, the suits, the shoes and gear bags. No more than the players, Sean had it down to a fine art at that stage, because this was the sixth All-Ireland final he had prepared us for.

Once again, the crowds were turning out in huge numbers to watch us train in Dalgan Park, and that always gave me a bit of an extra pep in my step. The build-up was good, training was no different to what it had been and we had no injuries ahead of the game. We were in a good place.

Mayo had beaten Kerry in their semi-final. Looking at that game - and looking at how we'd beaten Tyrone – I have to be honest and say I thought we were going to beat Mayo comfortably. I'll put my hand up and admit that. Even after the performance we had put in against Tyrone, I thought there was even more in us. I didn't think people had even seen the best of us yet, and I thought we'd put in an even better display against Mayo.

I was sitting down with Colm Coyle one night, because we were the two elder statesmen, and I said all that to him. He turned around to me.

'Martin... you know All-Ireland finals aren't won easy.'

That made me think for a second.

I SAID TO myself that I better get that idea out of my head fairly quickly, because this could be a big battle. Not for the first time in his life, Coyler was right; it wasn't won easy. I totally changed my frame of mind at training and started telling lads that this was going to be tough. When you look at 1990 and the way we underestimated Cork in that game, maybe I hadn't fully learned my lesson.

My thinking was that I felt our game with Tyrone was 100 miles an hour, whereas the Mayo-Kerry game was about 60 miles an hour. That was how it looked to me. Also, when it came to the match-ups, I never for a second thought that Pat Holmes was going to play on Graham Geraghty. I didn't think he'd be able to handle Graham, but Pat Holmes was a sticky marker and he did a great job on the day.

For the drawn game, we were both wearing green. I think someone in Croke Park, or whoever makes these decisions, should have told us to wear the Leinster colours and told Mayo to wear the Connacht colours. When we played Mayo in the 1988 'semi', we wore gold jerseys and they wore red. When we played Donegal in the 1990 'semi', we wore Leinster colours and they wore Ulster colours. Same with Kerry in 1986 – we both changed.

The jerseys in 1996 were very similar, the design was the same except for Mayo's hoop. They had red on the shoulders and we had gold. So it was a bit confusing for me. I used to kick the ball to the opposition a good bit anyway, but I'm blaming the jerseys on this occasion!

WE WERE FOUR points down with 10 minutes to go in that first game, and we couldn't get going at all. It was a fairly breezy day. Mayo started better and went a couple of points up. We really struggled to get our game going and we were 0-7 to 0-4 down at half-time. Ten minutes into the second-half, a long ball came into our full-back line.

Darren Fay and Paddy Reynolds both went for it and got in each other's way. Next thing the ball broke, and Ray Dempsey came in and side-footed it past Conor Martin. So that was us six points down and playing terribly. I thought that was it. Mayo would only score one more point after that though, and we chipped away.

One point, then another, then another.

We had pulled it back to a single point with time almost up. Then came the famous score from Colm Coyle which levelled things up.

Coyler got it around the middle of the field, beside that coloured patch they started putting on the pitch for All-Irelands. He drove in what could only be described as a *Hail Mary* ball. That was the only thing for it at that stage – put it in there and hope for a lucky break. Somehow Mark O'Reilly – who was a corner-back – was up there and he almost got his hand to it and put it in the net. It could have gone anywhere. It managed to miss everyone in the goalmouth and bounced clean over the bar.

The final whistle went soon after. We got out of jail. It was a really poor showing that day and we never clicked at all. We had no rhythm to our game. The best thing about it was the way we came back after going six down. Brendan Reilly got a couple of great points, Trevor Giles kicked his frees, John McDermott got one - then there was that last score from Colm which saved us.

It was hard to know why we played so badly. After playing so well four weeks earlier, then to have this performance – it was hard to explain. Training had gone well, everyone was in good form, and there were no injuries, nothing. Maybe, deep down, lads thought that they were going to win comfortably. Every dog on the street was telling us that we were going to win.

When people are saying that – and they mean well – it can get into your head, and it's very hard to get it out. Also, it must be said that Mayo were an awful lot better than we thought. They were a strong outfit and were very unlucky. It was a terrible Meath performance though, and Mayo could have been out of sight had they not kicked so many wides.

The lesson here might be to scrape through your All-Ireland semi-final by the skin of your teeth. When you look at what happened to us in 1996 and again in 2001 after impressive semi-finals, it probably doesn't help. We hammered Tyrone, and all of a sudden people were saying we're the best they'd ever seen. Definitely the best way to go into a final is to struggle through the semi-final and don't perform to your best, if you can do that.

Of course, it's not as simple as that. If we had produced that Tyrone performance in the final, it would have been fantastic. But, as Coyler said, it's not easily done.

After the drawn game, there was a huge sense of anti-climax. We went back to the hotel, headed home the next day, and then we were back training on the Tuesday. Believe you me, it takes a while to pick things up after a game like that. That first week back training, things were at an all-time low. It was torture training and trying to build ourselves back up again, because we thought we were done with it the week before. We had put so much effort in, then all of a sudden we're back training.

Everybody was really flat. There were obviously no celebrations the night of the drawn game, so everything was back to normal very quickly. It was a huge come-down and it took us a week to really get going again.

THAT WAS IN total contrast to the night of the 1988 drawn final, when we had a great time. Both games were very similar in that we didn't play well, and got out of jail right at the end. For some strange reason though, there was a totally different feel around the '96 draw, I'm not sure why.

It might have been down to the high of beating Tyrone and maybe thinking that we should beat Mayo. It might have been that in 1988 we knew we were going to have it tough against Cork and we were glad to get a second chance, whereas in '96 we might have been overconfident and we were brought back down to earth with a bang.

We knew that we'd got away with one, so it was back to the drawing board and back to training to try and make sure we put in a better performance the second day. We had a chat on the Monday morning about what went wrong and what we needed to do better. It took about two or three training sessions to get that game out of our system and focus on the next day.

For the replay, we came out in the yellow shirts and green shorts. I thought we should wear white shorts, while Sean thought we should wear green. Myself, Tommy Dowd and Colm Coyle were asked after the drawn game what colours we should wear in the replay? I said yellow shirts and white shorts.

We were training in Gormonston in the lead-up to the replay, and Tommy would always pick me up. We'd always have a great laugh on the way to and from training. If that car could talk! One evening we were coming home, and Sean was after mentioning the colours of the togs to Tommy, and asking him what colour he thought we should wear?

Tommy, being captain, asked myself and Coyler what we thought, and we both said white shorts. Tommy rang Sean to tell him this. Sean had other ideas! About 10 minutes after Tommy rang Sean, my phone rang. It was Sean – like a divil.

'I hear ye want to wear white shorts? What about black ones!?'

I said that I didn't care what ones we wore as long as we won. We played in the green shorts in the end. But I laughed at Sean ringing me up about it. It wouldn't have been like him to lose the cool, especially over something like that. It just showed how on edge everyone was about the replay, and how determined everyone was to do better.

Colm Brady had come on in the drawn game and had done well, so he started the replay instead of Evan Kelly. That was the first time the starting 15 had been changed that whole championship. We wore those Donegal colours as I call them and, six minutes in, all hell broke loose. The conditions that day were probably the worst I had ever played in. I don't mind it being wet and a bit breezy, but this was a gale-force wind, the sun was shining, and there was feck all rain.

The wind was horrible. It was blowing straight down into Hill 16 at the time. Early in the game, Maurice Sheridan had a free from under the Cusack Stand. It wasn't really kickable for a right-footer, and it dropped short into the goal-mouth. I had it in my hands for a second before John McDermott took it.

He was coming out with it, and Anthony Finnerty came in and hit McDermott a little slap in the face. I came in and pushed Finnerty out of the way and then…chaos!

People will say to me, 'You hit nobody' or 'You hit this fella'.

Actually, I hit nobody, and nobody hit me.

At first I was running around trying to stop lads fighting, because there were only one or two at it, initially. Then all of a sudden there were four or five lads involved, then very quickly there were 20 lads at it.

I was fed up running around trying to stop fights, because what would surely have happened is I'd get a box myself, and I'd end up in the middle of it. The handiest way out for me was to go up to the umpire, who was Francie McMahon. Francie was a driver for Manor Farm chickens, and I used to meet him on the road regularly.

So I said to Francie, 'What's going to happen here?'

'Colm Coyle and Liam McHale are going to be sent off,' he told me.

How those two were going to be picked out, I don't know. That's what Francie said, Lord have mercy on him, and he was right. I was chatting to him for a couple of minutes and there wasn't a chicken or a ham mentioned!

'How can you pick those two?' I asked him.

I mean, lads were milling each other, but I didn't realise it was so bad until I saw it on the television. It took a while to calm down, but I don't think there were too many decent boxes thrown, though Colm threw a few, I'd say!

So, Pat McEnaney came in to chat to Francie and I walked away. Pat came out, sent the two boys off, and that was it. I know he said many years later in an interview that he was going to send off McHale and John McDermott until he spoke to Francie, who had spotted Coyler 'dropping six of them'. So that's what happened.

WHY THERE WAS a melee, I don't know.

Maybe we were overhyped, or we wanted to prove a point? It's hard to say. There had never been any niggle between ourselves and Mayo in any of our previous meetings. This was much worse than what happened between ourselves and Cork, even though there was a lot of bad blood between us back in 1987 and '88.

A lot of people were saying that we lost our worst player and Mayo lost their best. I don't go along with that for a second. Coyler was a huge loss to us. I thought he had been excellent that year. He played well in the drawn game and he added a bit of steel to our defence. On top of that, he had two younger lads with him in the half-back line, and now he was gone.

I was left on my own with a lot of inexperienced lads around me. So Colm was a big loss not just for his football ability, but also for his experience and his talking on the field. Mind you, those young lads came of age that day.

The game settled down after the row, but shortly after that I was backing up to catch a ball, and I pulled something in my hip. My God, it was sore, but I battled on. I wasn't going to give in, but I was black and blue that night. I did okay in that game, though the conditions were terrible for both sides and it was a really difficult wind to play into. I picked up one of the few bookings I can remember getting in my career later in the half. I caught a ball under the Cusack Stand and passed it over Maurice Sheridan's head. He body-checked me slightly, and I pushed him back. The ref booked the two of us.

I had been marking Ray Dempsey early on, but he was taken off about 10 minutes before half-time. PJ Loftus came in, who was a bit of a speed merchant. He wasn't long on the field when a high ball came in between Mark O'Reilly and Anthony Finnerty. I could see it was going to break either left or right, so I went one way, but the ball went the other.

I was within touching distance of Loftus, and I could have pulled him down, but I knew that if I did I'd be sent off. He stuck it in the top corner with a great finish. That put Mayo six points up with half-time approaching.

Again though, we were able to hit back straight away, which was a real trait of the Meath teams I played on.

We got a penalty after a long ball was played into the Mayo square and Tommy was dragged down. Trevor stepped up and stuck it away, so the Mayo goal was cancelled out almost immediately. That probably knocked the stuffing out of them a small bit. If they had tagged on one or two points after getting their goal, it could have been curtains for us. As it was, we went in just four points behind, which wasn't too bad given the wind Mayo had in the first-half.

They struggled a bit for scores after half-time because of the gale that was there. James Horan took a shot at one stage and I was right behind him. It was going straight over the bar, and the wind just took it and it dropped short. At the other end, Trevor floated over a few great points that the wind helped carry over. You could just put the ball up and the wind would nearly do the rest.

In spite of having the elements behind us, we were still behind by two points with around 10 minutes to go. That was when Tommy Dowd played a captain's part and popped up with a vital goal. Graham won a free, which would have been one that Trevor would have knocked over at his ease. I'd say the Mayo defence were thinking the same, and they dropped their guard for a split second.

Graham took it quickly to Tommy, who was unmarked around the 21 yard line. Tommy rounded the goalkeeper, fell on the ground, and how he got his leg to it to kick it I don't know - but he rolled it into the net.

It was a dour game, and we were lucky to win by one thanks to Brendan Reilly's famous point down at the Hill 16 end. He turned his man, took a touch, and stuck it over from an impossible angle. He didn't drill it, he just curled it and the wind took it in.

Mayo came back at us again right at the end - down the Hogan Stand side. Someone got a half-block on a shot and the ball broke to me. I got around my man and I drove it as far as I could. Then I heard the final whistle. We hadn't played well at all. Were we lucky to win it? We probably were a little. Mayo actually played better against the wind than we did, they carried the ball a little bit better even though the winning point came from Colm McManamon carrying the ball into trouble and getting dispossessed.

I REALLY VALUED that one, and took everything in.

I didn't go too mad, and relished every minute. We were back in The Davenport Hotel after the game and met everyone there. I would say I enjoyed that one more than the other two. People sometimes ask me did it make up for losing in 1990 and '91?

It doesn't. Nothing makes up for losing an All-Ireland final, because you can't get them back, no matter how many more you win. I was lucky enough to go on and win that third medal, as was Coyler. Other lads weren't so lucky. It wasn't a classic, and we certainly didn't play the way we did against Tyrone, but that game was played on a perfect day for football and we were well up for it.

The two games against Mayo were really dogged, desperate games. The replay especially was a desperate spectacle for a final, not helped by the conditions. It felt to me like the two teams brought the worst out of one another.

I wouldn't have been as close to the lads on the 1996 team as I would be with the 1987-88 team, but there was a strong bond there – we saw that when they went on and won another All-Ireland in 1999. It was different for me in '96 because I was the older lad in among a lot of young lads. I was coming to the end, and I'd spent so much time with the previous team, whereas the young lads wouldn't have spent much time with the old guard at all.

A few like Tommy, Trevor, McDermott, McGuinness and some others would have, but the lads who had only just come in in 1996 wouldn't have. So I wouldn't have spent as much time with a lot of those lads as I would have with Mick, Gerry Mc and Colm. It was only natural that you'd feel closer to lads who you spent more time with. But the bond was still great. You don't win All-Irelands unless you have that, no matter what age you are.

I suppose the fact that a lot of lads joined in the melee showed we were a tight-knit bunch! Why it kicked off, I really don't know. To this day I'm puzzled by it. It made us look bad, because there was all the controversy with me over the incident in the Tyrone game. Then a month later, Meath are involved in another skirmish and everyone seemed to hate us. It was a pity, because I don't think any team deserves that.

But those two incidents so near to one another – it didn't do the county or the team any good. We had no choice but to take it in our stride and get on with it.

The next day, when the dust settled – or so we thought – both teams were brought back to Croke Park for a function. You could cut the tension with a knife. There were two buses leaving our hotel – the team bus and the supporters' bus. Sean had tickets for the function to hand out to the team. But between one thing and another, some of the team went on the supporters' bus, and some of the supporters went on the team bus, so everything was mixed up.

The first bus went about five minutes before the second. I was with Tommy Dowd and Colm Coyle on the second bus, and Tommy had the Sam Maguire Cup. The first bus landed at Croke Park and everybody went in. Then we arrived, and there were stewards and Croke Park blazers outside, and we couldn't get in. The lads in the green jackets wouldn't let us in because we had no tickets, and we had no tickets because Sean was gone in with all of them! He was above looking down on us.

We had the Sam Maguire Cup, and Meath blazers on, and yet we couldn't get in.

We couldn't get in for love nor money.

Eventually Sean got word as to what was going on, so he came down and handed out the tickets, and in we went.

There was a bit of friction between players from both teams, and words were said. The President of the GAA got up to say a few words and Sean said a few words. Next, it was John Maughan's turn. He never congratulated us properly, I felt. He spoke about how great the Mayo team was – which you would expect – then at the very end he just said, 'Well done Meath'.

That didn't go down too well. There was a bad atmosphere across that whole function, and it raised its head at different times. I saw a few of the Mayo lads at the All Stars do a few months later, but there was no talk with them or Tyrone. I don't know if they didn't want to talk to us or we didn't want to talk to them, or both! There seemed to be a real hatred there, worse than what we had with Cork, I would say. I haven't seen any of the Mayo lads since, but I'm sure if I was over there and I bumped into any of them, they'd chat to me and we'd have the craic.

Jack Boothman was the GAA president at the time, and he just brushed it off during his speech at that function. He was very diplomatic about it, he didn't really make any issue of things. He mentioned that the brawl was something that shouldn't have happened, but he passed over it and moved on, which was in total contrast to what happened with John Dowling in 1988.

After the 1996 final, a lot of suspensions were handed out. Jimmy McGuinness got the longest suspension – six months. You would think someone was after being killed. I thought the whole thing was blown out of proportion. Jimmy was highlighted on *The Sunday Game*, and Pat Spillane mentioned that he was like Michael Flatley. Jimmy got involved early in the row, and by the time it finished I think he was nearly under the Cusack Stand. He wasn't going for a walk either, he hit everything going! Maybe six months wasn't that outrageous now that I think of it!

We got a lot of bad publicity after 1988 and '96, but it didn't bother us. The more bad press we got, the more motivated we were. I really think a lot of teams who came after us modelled themselves on those Meath sides.

CHAPTER **19**

SUNDAY, OCTOBER 9, 2005

CLASS HAS NO 'USE-BY' DATE

"Last Sunday, local heroes took the stage to bring honour and glory to their home places. It is a time when club players care little about who won the All-Ireland. This is the real beauty of the GAA. In Down, Mickey Linden won another senior medal at the age of 42 with Mayobridge. A great county man for years, a great club man forever. In Navan, another hero of heroes, Martin O'Connell, won a Junior championship medal with St Michael's, 23 years after he won his previous one. Many of the team were not even born when he won that first medal. Two of those men who played last week are nephews of mine, John Barry and Felim O'Reilly, and I was very proud that they played a part in the win. But the day belonged to the man with eternal youth. Passion is the most important ingredient of success and O'Connell always had that; he also had a love of place and a pride in his club. He could have joined any senior team he wanted, but loyalty and modesty were his middle names. And those players from last week will realise in time, if they don't know it already, that they were privileged to have shared a dressing-room with one of the greatest Meath players of the last 100 years – and I will throw in the next 100 as well."

Colm O'Rourke
The Sunday Independent

FINISHING MY CLUB career on a high was something that was really important to me, and I was very lucky that worked out that way. Dudley Farrell was over us in 2005, and he asked me if I would go back for another year. I said I'd have a think about it and, for the first time ever, I didn't go back training in January or February.

My body was starting to cave in a bit, so I sat out those early months. I was doing a small bit myself, trying to keep myself in shape, then Dudley rang me again in March or April and I went back in. I was delighted to get back training with the lads. Understandably, I didn't start in the first couple of championship games, but I got back in soon enough and I went from there. I felt we had a good chance of winning the Junior that year because we had a few good young lads coming through. We had Felim and JB O'Reilly, Johnny Reilly, Ciarán Lynch – who represented the county at Junior level – and Daithí 'Scaldy' Regan, who was playing with Meath around that time.

So we had a good crop of younger lads and then I added a bit of experience. I think the half-forward line in that Junior final was Johnny Reilly, who was 17, Felim who was 17, and me who was 42! So, we had a bit of experience and a lot of legs. I saw the lads in training so I knew we had a chance.

We played against St Ultan's in the group stages in Simonstown. One particular moment sticks out in my mind from that game. Everyone gives out about referees, but a fella called Gerry McGivney was refereeing this game and I have to give him a bit of praise. I went up in the middle of three or four lads and came down with the ball.

I was surrounded by two or three of them, but nobody laid a hand on me. Next thing, the whistle goes and the referee gave me a free. I looked at him slightly surprised, and he looked back and said, 'Anyone who can catch a ball like that deserves a free!'

It was the nicest thing a referee ever said to me!

I took it quickly, and Scaldy stuck it in the net, which turned the game on its head. I think we won by three or four in the end. I hope the Ultan's lads didn't hear the ref's comments, because I don't think they'd have been too happy! So the lesson there is, if you catch a ball between three or four lads, you'll get the free if Gerry is doing the game!

Once I was back training, I wanted my place back. The old competitiveness came to the surface quickly enough and I didn't want to be sitting on the line watching. By the time the quarter-final came around, I was back on the '40'. My body was holding up fairly well and I had no injuries. The back and hamstrings were at me a small bit, but I wasn't going at 100 miles an hour anymore. I wasn't sprinting full-tilt.

I had learned to push myself just enough, but not to the point where I was going to break down. We met Dunsany – who were always there or thereabouts in the Junior championship – in the quarter-final. Scaldy rescued us with a late free in that game to level it, and we won the replay by three points. The semi-final was a local derby against Kilmainham in Kells, and I think we all expected that to be a tight enough game. We had the ball in the net three times in the first 10 minutes, which basically put that game to bed. We won easily enough in the end. I twanged my hamstring just a little at the end of that one, and the final was in two weeks, so I had to mind myself during that fortnight.

I used to wear the bicycle shorts, and had a lot of strapping on me for most games at that stage, but I was like a mummy going out for that final against Navan O'Mahonys!

THE MORNING OF that final and going to the game is something that stays with me, because it was as good as an All-Ireland morning. I was living outside Navan, where I still am today, so I'd only be 10 minutes from Páirc Tailteann.

Martin Stafford, who was a great clubman, said to me, 'Sure there's no point in you coming all the way over to the club, we'll see you in Navan'. But, I really wanted to go from the club with the lads. So Martin came down, collected me and brought me over to the clubhouse in Carlanstown.

We were all getting a bus into Navan and I wanted to be part of that. I stopped in the shop on the way to the club and got my usual pink snack, got to the clubhouse and met the lads. I had elephants in my stomach, and me 42! The bus came and there were lots of people out wishing us well and seeing us off. It was every bit as good as an All-Ireland final, because it was really near the end for me, so the thoughts of winning and finishing with a Junior title really gave me a buzz.

We had new tops, gear bags and the little extras that make getting to a final so special. We didn't get any suits, but never mind!

I was confident that we'd win, because we had a good bunch of lads with a good attitude. Dudley was an excellent trainer so we were well-drilled and very fit. The fact that it was against O'Mahony's helped us, too. The big town team against the country village. Any rural club would tell you they always love taking on the town clubs.

I knew most of the O'Mahony's team, because they were lads who had all played Senior in previous years – most of them anyway. We knew we were going to be up against it, but playing O'Mahony's in Navan was a huge incentive. The support we had that day was huge – we outnumbered them by 10 to 1. Maybe because they were a Senior club, they didn't think much of the Junior, but there seemed to be very few of their supporters at that game.

I played okay in that final. I would say I was solid, if not spectacular. Scaldy and John Farrell got the goals for us and Ciarán Lynch got a few scores, too. For us to win that game, Scaldy needed to play well – and he did. He got 1-5 out of 2-11 for us, which was vital. He was a super player, but he gave it up shortly after that and it was a pity he did. He's back playing now, but it's 10 years too late. Lads make their own decisions for their own reasons, so I wouldn't ever knock that.

I was marking Cathal Ó Bric, who was an old-stager like myself, and he was hard enough to get away from. He played a lot of Senior football for Navan O'Mahony's but was coming to the end so was playing Junior with them that year. I tried to pull him out of the centre so our lads could run down the middle and create chances. I knew that if I went to the toilet, Ó Bric would follow me because he was a tight marker.

I was 42 at that stage, so he was probably a little bit naïve in following me. He should have had enough experience to know better. So I pulled out to the wing and he'd follow me, and I think the two goals we got that day came from me not being in the centre. I only really got one chance myself, which I kicked wide, so I just focused on trying to set up other lads and keep the ball moving.

Johnny 'The Lamb' Reilly did a lot of running for us that day aswell. We called him 'The Lamb' because he had an older brother called 'The Sheep', but 'Sheep' had given up at that stage! Overall, I was probably just there to help them out. A huge loss to us for that final was Tom Halpin. He was sent off in the semi-final against Kilmainham, so missed out due to suspension. Tom was a great servant to the club, and played with the county aswell. For him to miss out at that stage of his career – he was an experienced player with not as long left as some of the other lads – was tough. I felt bad for him because I felt he was sent off in the wrong in the semi-final.

Running out in Páirc Tailteann that day, I had more or less made my mind up that this was going to be it for me – win or lose. I was starting to tighten up a bit and get the odd injury, so I said that if we won that match, I'd give the Leinster Junior club championship a rattle and then call it a day. Athy beat us in that competition in Carlanstown.

Coming off the field, I took a look back at the pitch and thought to myself… *That's me done.* That was my last competitive game for St Michael's – until I stood in the goals five or six years later because we only had 14 for a game!

THERE WAS A great sense of satisfaction after the final whistle went in that Junior final. To win was just fantastic, and the homecoming was even better. We had a big 'do' in Simonstown and a bit of food there, then we were back on the bus to Carlanstown and we were met with bonfires. The roads were all blocked off, and we had a big trailer that we all got up on to say a few words.

I held up traffic in Carlanstown three times when I was playing with Meath after we won All-Irelands and had a homecoming, but to do it after winning a Junior with your own club was hard to beat.

I didn't get too jarred because I wanted to take it all in.

The young lads enjoyed themselves because it was their first time and they were having the craic, but I just sat back and made the best of the celebrations. It was brilliant, better than an All-Ireland in many ways.

To see the happiness it brought to so many was what really made it for me. My father had put so much into the club over the years, and thankfully he's still going strong. John Moran, Martin Stafford, Paddy McIntyre, Petesy Cassidy… you could go on and on, naming lads and I've probably left someone out, but it was great to win something for those lads. I was lucky because my club career started out with success, and it ended with success.

I was centre-forward in 1982, and centre-forward in '05. It proved that it was the right thing to do to amalgamate the two clubs all those years ago.

As much as I said I was done after that game against Athy, I tried to get back again in 2006. Unfortunately, I just wasn't able. I always feel that every now and again, there's an easy championship to be won. When I say easy, I don't mean easy in the true sense of the word. But every now and again you'll look at a championship at the start of a season and think that it's wide open, and any team who gets their act together could win it. That was what

I thought about that 2006 Intermediate. Rathkenny beat Drumconrath in the final that year, and I thought it was there for the taking for a few teams – including ourselves. I thought that maybe if I could get back, I could help the team, but it wasn't to be.

The body wasn't able. Your mind will tell you that you can still do everything, but the body isn't long telling you that you can't.

WHEN I FINISHED with the county, I took it very badly, so giving up football altogether was tough to take and took me a year or so to get over. Going to games and seeing the lads playing, thinking you should be out there... that wasn't easy. It didn't take me as long to get over finishing with the club as it did with the county, but it was still a jolt because this was something I had been doing since I was a child, and was part of my life.

I always wanted to give a bit back, so I managed St Michael's for a couple of years. We got to an Intermediate quarter-final but were beaten by St Colmcille's. That was as far as we went. When I was managing the club, I thought back to what Mick Lyons had said when he was involved as a selector with Meath. I found it difficult to go in and manage lads that I knew and that I had played with.

I didn't want to make any enemies, so I had to be careful with what I said. There were things I wanted to say, but I didn't feel like I could.

I'm involved with Walterstown now and they were a Senior club for years, but now they're Intermediate. So if you don't put the work in, that's what can happen.

When you look at why Meath football has gone back so much in the last 20 years, I think it's down to underage coaching structures. I came out of the 2001 All-Ireland final after Galway had beaten us, and I don't know why but I said to Samantha, 'That defeat will set us back 20 years'. I don't think the underage structures were what they should have been. Certainly it's better now.

The game itself has changed a lot, of course. When I played, there were one-on-one battles all over the field. The full-back against the full-forward, centre-back and centre-forward. Every man looked to win his own battle.

That's pretty much gone from the game now.

It reminds me a bit of basketball in that if a team loses the ball, they all drop back into defence. The crowd are shouting the let the ball in, but often there's nobody to let it in to. I find I'm bored watching a lot of the games today. Having said that, I love the game and the GAA as a whole. The way it's gone now, would I like to be 20 and starting off in the modern era?

I'd love to. The only problem is, I'd have to get up at 6.0 am to train. I don't think that would suit me and I don't think there's any need for it. I was training five nights a week between Meath and my own stuff. We did Tuesday, Thursday, Saturday and Sunday with Meath, and then I did my own stuff on Wednesday. I might have gone to Bettystown or into Navan Racecourse for a run, or some sprints in the back garden.

When the two boys – Brian and Barry – came along, I would always have been keen for them to play. The same with my daughter, Jane. She's heavily involved, too. I wouldn't have put any pressure on them to play, but I wanted them to at least try it because I think football is great for young people. Not just for sporting and health reasons, but also for the people you meet. You could batter someone on the field for an hour and then shake hands and have a pint after.

I had no trouble getting the lads into it, they loved it from day one. I was always hoping they would, and they had a bit of success underage with Walterstown, and now they're playing Intermediate football. Barry was in with the Meath under 17s and Brian had a few runs with the minors. Barry would be more like me, football would be big for him. Brian would be a bit more relaxed, he could take it or leave it.

I think he takes after his mother!

WHEN I LOOK back on my career, there are a few things that stick out. The buzz I used to get going into Croke Park is just something, I'll never forget. In the early days, we used to meet in Ashbourne and drive in, and the drive was unbelievable. When you got into Croke Park and walked onto the pitch and looked at the stadium – that was always magic.

I loved running out onto the field and hearing the cheers and the shouting from the crowd.

We would do our stretching inside in the dressing-room. This was before the huge warm-up area, that's there now. We'd get in our lines when we got onto the field and do maybe 10 minutes of a warm-up. I see a lot of cones and drills before games now and I wonder how lads have the energy to play a game at all.

There was nothing too complex that Sean would say to us before games. The talks on Tuesday and Thursday before games would be more intense.

The watch would come off, and the room would go silent.

EPILOGUE

THERE WAS NO announcement when I left the Meath panel for the second and final time. No Twitter or Instagram posts, no statement released via the GPA.

None of those outlets existed at the time, of course, but even if they had, that wasn't how things were done. Mick Lyons always said, 'When you retire… just go. Don't announce it in the papers, don't announce it on radio… just go.'

So I think everyone had that in their head – you just go.

Don't make a fuss.

That would have been in keeping with the way Meath teams of that era went about their business. I had a few phone calls from journalists at the time, but I just have told them that I wasn't retired, I'm still playing with my club.

If the county needs me, they know where I am.

I found it very hard to let go of being a Meath footballer, and I held out hope that I might get back in again. I thought I might have received a call in 1999, because there was a spell when the squad was a bit light with injuries and illness. So when anyone asked me about my career, I would never have said, 'I've retired from county football', because I thought maybe, just maybe, I might get the call again.

Tommy Dowd was injured in 1999, but came on for a couple of minutes at the end of the All-Ireland final, just to be a part of it. When I saw him coming on, I couldn't help thinking that maybe I could have had the same farewell.

It wasn't to be. There were no hard feelings with anyone though. I had to take it on the chin and move on, as hard as that was. I had been a sub in 1998 but hadn't played. Maybe I could have done the same in '99, too, but that was never me. I wouldn't have been one to sit on the bench for a couple of years at the end, regardless of what success the team had.

Having played for so long, I wouldn't have been able to just make up the numbers. It was better that I went when I did.

If I had my time again, I probably would have made some kind of statement. It would have been nice to get a few headlines and do some interviews, but it just wasn't the done thing back then. We all just drifted away.

New players come in, new heroes emerge, and the memory of those who came before slowly fades.

✦ ✦ ✦ ✦ ✦ ✦ ✦ ✦

TUESDAY, AUGUST 10, 1999

IF I FELT that I had missed out on some recognition by not formally announcing my retirement, I got it a year later in slightly surprising circumstances.

An Post and the GAA had decided to mark the arrival of the year 2000 by announcing a Team of the Millennium. A panel made up of four former GAA Presidents (Dr. Mick Loftus, Peter Quinn, Paddy McFlynn and Jack Boothman) and six journalists (Donal Carroll, Paddy Downey, Mick Dunne, Paddy O'Hara, Mícheál Ó Muircheartaigh and Raymond Smith) plus then-GAA Director General Liam Mulvihill were given the fairly difficult job of picking the best 15 Gaelic footballers in the history of the game.

The whole thing generated a lot of publicity over the course of about six weeks, as *The Irish Independent* published pen pictures of the nominees for each position every Monday, Wednesday and Friday. In total, 120 players were nominated, and members of the public were invited to submit their own personal 15.

There were nine Meath players nominated. Bob O'Malley, Mick O'Brien, Paddy O'Brien, Pat Reynolds, Gerry McEntee, Colm O'Rourke, Peter McDermott, Bernard Flynn and myself.

The date when the team was to be announced was mentioned in the paper regularly, so I knew when it was happening. A week or so before it was due to be revealed, I got a phone call from someone in Croke Park. I was told to be there the following Tuesday. Given that there were 120 lads nominated, I assumed it was going to be like an All Star 'do'. I thought we'd all be brought up and it would be a fairly glitzy event. I had visions of The Burlington, black-tie, nice dinner and all the rest. Sure this was going to be a great night with the lads! It didn't quite pan out that way.

I picked up the phone and rang a few of the boys to see what the story was. Colm hadn't heard anything from Croke Park, nor had Bob. Bernard Flynn and Gerry Mc hadn't had any call either. I was a bit surprised to hear that, and then I nearly felt bad for having called them in the first place! Not that bad mind you, just a little bit!

Driving up to Croke Park with Samantha that day, I didn't really know what to expect. It was a Tuesday afternoon and the championships were still in full swing. Cork had narrowly beaten Offaly in the All-Ireland hurling semi-final the previous Sunday. Meath were still involved too, of course, and had beaten Dublin comfortably in the Leinster final 10 days before.

That was the day when Ollie Murphy kicked 1-5, including a beautiful goal into the Hill. Everyone's minds were still focused on what was happening on the field. You would have thought that something like a Team of the Millennium announcement would be done when the season was over. Regardless of that, I was delighted to be heading up.

When I got to Croke Park, being honest, I was fairly disappointed. We went into the Hogan Stand, but the place wasn't decked out in any way. There were just a few tables here and there, in one of the function rooms.

It wasn't what I had expected at all.

It was very low-key. I had expected a big crowd and lots of noise, but we just walked in and took a seat. The other players who were nominated were there. A few of the older guys had passed away, so their families were there to represent them.

I REALISED THAT I was going to be on the team, as it seemed none of the other nominees for my position were there. We had a bit of grub and afterwards Mícheál Ó Muircheartaigh called out the team.

'Left-half-back… Martin O'Connell.'

It was great to be named, and I was very excited to be there, but I thought the whole event should have been done like an All Star night. Make a big deal out of it. After the team was announced, a few of us went out onto the field with our framed portraits for some photos for the following day's papers.

Like the handful of players who stood on the field with me, Croke Park had changed almost beyond recognition from our days as players. But for all the changes that the years had brought, we were still the same men with the same heart and soul, and Croke Park still had the same heart and soul, in spite of the facelift.

The memories came drifting back. Good and bad. The drive in, the Garda escorts. Bursting out of the dressing-room and onto the pitch for another big game.

It became routine.

The colour, the noise.

There's the spot in the corner where the move for Foley's goal started in 1991. Me just about keeping the ball in, picking it up and passing it to Mick.. The final that year, and not getting back to Barry Breen until it was too late.

All-Ireland wins.

All-Ireland defeats.

The noise of the crowd for the 1996 semi-final.

Hill 16.

The row with Mayo.

The steps of the Hogan. All the times I'd been up them.

The 1994 league final which felt like an All-Ireland.

All the times when I didn't quite make it.

The dugouts.

It was hard to separate the good memories from the bad.

I STOOD ALONGSIDE Seán Purcell, Pat Spillane, Kevin Heffernan, Mick O'Connell and Enda Colleran. I'm sure the lads would all have been running through their own memories as they stood and smiled.

I was slightly embarrassed that I was named and some of my teammates weren't, when you look at some of the names. It's like picking a team, there's always controversy. You could probably pick 10 different teams.

There are lads not on that team who you could say should be on it. One would be Jack O'Shea. I grew up looking at him playing football and he was the best midfielder I'd ever seen. I thought Jacko should have been on it, and maybe Brian Mullins aswell. But the left half-back position – and I'm not being humble – was probably an easier position to get picked.

When I saw the nominees, I thought I had a chance.

I don't think I was the best player that played for Meath. You had Colm O'Rourke, Gerry McEntee, Bob O'Malley, Mick Lyons... you could name plenty more. But look, it wasn't my fault I got on it!

WE WENT BACK inside after the photos were taken.

I was chatting to Pat Spillane and one or two others, and I went up to the bar to get a drink, only to find that the bar was closed! That summed up the day for me.

It felt like they wanted us out of there as soon as possible once the formalities were out of the way and the photos were taken. That was a bit of a kick in the backside. I would love to have stayed up overnight with everyone and had a good catch-up with the lads. But Spillane was heading home to Kerry. So was Mikey Sheehy.

We chatted for a while and then said, 'Look, I'll see you again', and we went our separate ways. Myself and Samantha decided to head home aswell.

As we were leaving, we bumped into Brendan Cummins, the well-known

Meath GAA official and local radio commentator with *LMFM*. I did a bit of an interview with him. Brian Carthy from RTÉ grabbed me for a quick chat, too. He had Sean Boylan on the phone, who wasn't able to make it in for some reason.

Brian handed me the phone and I had a quick chat with Sean. He was really happy for me and very proud. He said some nice things so it was great to speak to him at a time like that. We decided to go for a drink, so me, Brendan and Samantha went to Tolka House in Glasnevin. It wasn't quite how I imagined the day ending – in Tolka House at three o'clock in the afternoon!

It was three pints, then home.

I called out to see my parents, to give them the news. They were probably more thrilled than I was. There was a stamp commissioned for every fella who was on the team. A few weeks later, I got a letter in the post with my stamp on it from Bob O'Malley.

That was the first letter that came in the door with my head on it. No better man than Bob to think of doing something like that. It was a nice touch.

A few people were giving out that I shouldn't have my head on a stamp – they said my head was too big to fit on an envelope!

There were plenty who probably wanted to slap it rather than lick it, so I got a bit of slagging, but it was a nice thing to have. Not too many can say they had a stamp with their face on it. I still have a few of them, and I have the framed picture that we were given. That's hanging on the wall at home.

I never really thought about why I was named on that team, or why I was even nominated. As a player, I would always have tried to attack, at least when the legs would allow it. I was a good tackler, and I wasn't a dirty player. I had enough lads around me who could do that, and someone had to play a bit of ball!

I wouldn't have been a great passer. I gave the ball away a lot. You can ask any of the forwards about that, they didn't get too many balls on a plate, but it was no harm for some of them to fight for a ball now and again – especially Flynn!

Fielding, tackling, kicking the odd score... they'd have been my best attributes. I didn't dwell too long on the award at the time, because I was still playing with the club. As the years have passed, I've grown to appreciate it more.

I realise that I was lucky to have played on teams with so many great players and to have won so much. Along with my first All-Ireland, being on the Team of the Millennium was probably the highest honour I could get. I wouldn't have been one to sit down and think about what I've won.

Now I've a bit of time, I can do that.

I wasn't a flashy player or one who was in the limelight much. I took my football seriously, maybe too seriously at times, and kept the head down. In hindsight, maybe the low-key surroundings of Tolka House was the perfect place for that day in August '99 to end.

Brendan, Samantha and me.

Six Leinsters, three All-Irelands, three leagues.

Three pints, and home.

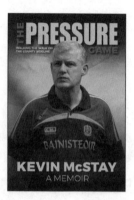

The Pressure Game
Kevin McStay: An Autobiography

For the first time one of the top GAA managers in the country has revealed the inside story of what it's like to 'Walk the Walk on a County Sideline'. Former Mayo Allstar footballer Kevin McStay gave up 20 years of working as a commentator and analyst on RTE's Sunday Game to take up the position of Roscommon team manager in 2016.

The whole country watched to see how he would survive on the sideline – and how he would face up to the pressures of facing Jim's Gavin's Dublin, Mayo and Kerry and Tyrone, on the toughest stage in Gaelic football.

In his three years in charge, McStay led Roscommon to a Connacht title in 2017 and a prized place in the Super 8s in 2018 before quitting the job. He has now returned to the RTE broadcasting booth.

This is the amazing inside story of the *The Pressure Game.*

Authors: Kevin McStay with Liam Hayes
Print Price: €20.00
Ebook: €10.00
ISBN: 9781910827086

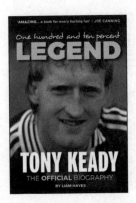

One Hundred and Ten Percent Legend
Tony Keady: The Official Biography

When Tony Keady died suddenly in August of 2017, at just 53 years of age, a whole county mourned and the rest of the country stopped in its tracks to say goodbye to a legend of the game of hurling.

Except Tony Keady was more than a legend.

In 1988, after leading Galway to a second All-Ireland title in succession, he was crowned the greatest hurler in Ireland. He was 25 years of age and there was nobody like him, nobody to touch him in the maroon No.6 shirt.

But, four years later, and still not 30, after being wrongly banned for 12 months by the GAA, he was also discarded by his own county and refused a maroon jersey the very last time he walked out onto Croke Park behind the Galway team.

A few months before his death, Tony Keady visited Liam Hayes and told him he wished to tell his own story. He felt it was time, but tragically time was not on Tony's side. One month after he died Galway won the All-Ireland title for the first time since 1988, and 80,000 people rose from their seats in the sixth minute of the game to applaud and remember a man who was more than a legend

Tony's wife, Margaret and his daughter, Shannon and his three boys, Anthony, Harry and Jake, decided to finish telling the story of a father and a hurler who always asked those around him for '110%.

Author: Liam Hayes
Price: €20.00
ISBN: 9781910827048

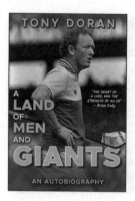

A Land of Men and Giants
The Tony Doran Autobiography

Wexford's All-Ireland winning hero Tony Doran was a giant in the game of hurling through the 1960s, 70s and 80s, at a time when full-forwards were ordered to plunder goals.

In his 19 years and 187 appearances as a Wexford hurler, Tony Doran successfully went for goal 131 times.

But Doran also played against giants from Kilkenny, Tipperary and Cork, and so many other counties, at a time when the game of hurling tested the wits and the courage of every man on the field.

Some of these men became giants.

A Land of Men and Giants is the story told by Tony Doran of a life spent living and competing against legendary men and true giants of the game.

A Land of Men and Giants: The Autobiography of Tony Doran is edited by award-winning writer and author Liam Hayes.

Authors: Tony Doran with Liam Hayes
Print Price: €20.00
ISBN: 9781910827031

Available on
Amazon

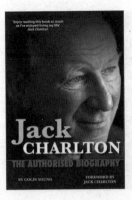

Jack Charlton
The Authorised Biography

As one of the true legends of Irish and English football, Jack Charlton was a man both loved and feared, but now the people who have lived with him all of his life introduce the real 'Big Jack' in this brilliant authorised biography which is presented in a foreword by Jack himself.

For the first time Jack's wife and family, his teammates as a World Cup winner with England in 1966, and his players during his management years with Middlesbrough, Sheffield Wednesday, Newcastle, and Ireland tell their stories of the man who dominated their lives.

Graeme Souness, Chris Waddle, and Peter Beardsley amongst others, are joined by Mick McCarthy, Niall Quinn and the greatest footballers who played under Big Jack for 10 years as Ireland team boss.

This is the most personable, inviting and intimate account of Jack Charlton's life, and the book contains photographs published for the first time from Jack and Pat Charlton's personal collection.

Jack Charlton: The Authorised Biography is written by former Daily Mail Northern Football Correspondent, Colin Young.

Authors: Colin Young
Print Price: €20.00
ISBN: 9781910827017

Available on
Amazon

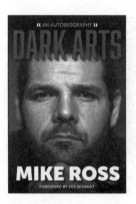

Dark Arts
Mike Ross: An Autobiography

For the first time, Mike Ross brings sports fans into the dark heart of the professional game of rugby union. Ross is recognised as the greatest scrummager in Irish rugby history – and the man who was the foundation stone for the beginning of the Joe Schmidt era, which saw Leinster win back-to-back Heineken Cups and Ireland become the greatest team in Europe.

But Mike Ross might never have been a professional rugby player. He did not turn pro until he was 26 years of age. And he spent three years learning his trade at the toughest end of the game with Harlequins in England before coming home at 30, and chasing the dream of an Irish jersey.

Ross would play 61 times for Ireland, and over 150 times for Leinster. His story is one of big dreams and amazing courage, on and off the field.

He writes about the good times and the hardest times, facing the true beasts of the professional game every weekend. And he writes about his own life, and the suicide of his younger brother, Andrew at 16 years of age with an honesty and compassion that is rewarding for everyone who has experienced the sudden death of a loved one and has to rebuild their lives.

Authors: Mike Ross with Liam Hayes
Print Price: €20.00
Ebook: €10.00
ISBN: 9781910827048

Available on
Amazon
Apple Books
Kobo
And all good online stores

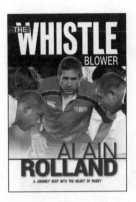

The Whistle Blower
The Alain Rolland Story

Alain Rolland is the only Irishman to have refereed a World Cup final.

Rolland's lifetime journey through the game – from Blackrock College to Leinster, to Ireland, and onto the greatest stage in rugby when he took charge of the 2007 World Cup final in the Stade de France between South Africa and England – brings readers deep into the heart of the professional game for the first time.

A former Leinster scrum-half, Rolland was capped 40 times for his province in the amateur era of the game, and also played three times for Ireland.

But it is as a referee that Alain Rolland is best known and respected throughout the world. In The Whistle Blower he now gives a unique and thrilling insight to the professional game, bringing readers up close with the 'Big Two' in Ireland, Leinster and Munster, and also allowing readers out onto the pitch with him as he travels the world and takes charge of the greatest teams in the game – Australia, South Africa and the mighty All Blacks.

Rolland's courage as a referee brought him fame and landed him deep in controversy on occasions. The Whistle Blower now explains his biggest decisions in life, and on the playing field.

Authors: Alain Rolland with Daragh O'Conchuir
Price: €20.00
ISBN: 9780952626022